Love Letters

Extraordinary Loving for Everyday Living

Paulette Dahl

Copyright © 2016 by Sharing Love Publications.

All rights reserved.

No part of this book may be copied, shared, referenced, or distributed without the written permission of the author or publisher.

ISBN: 978-0-9948437-0-8 (Paperback Book)

Cover Design: NZ Graphics
Design and Layout: WESType Publishing Services, Inc.

Inspirational, non-fiction, spiritual, personal growth & development, English

*Sending all of my Love 'n' Gratitude
to my sons and their partners:
Anthony Gras & Jeanine Middleton,
Christopher Gras & Britney St. Pierre, and
Gregory Gras & Rhya Repele.*

To Benton McLean: a dear Lover of Life.

*Most importantly,
I dedicate this book—and my life—to God,
the Divine Creator, who is the source of* all *Love!*

Contents

Preface	xi
Acknowledgements	xix
Introduction	xxvii
How To Use This Book	xxxi

Love Letters

From Loneliness	3
About Belonging	6
To Avoid Confusion	10
About Clarity	14
About the Grumpies	18
With Gratitude	22
From Depression	26
About Resilience	31

Love Letters

For Fatigue	35
To Passion	38
About Anger	41
To Inspire Peace	47
To Grief	51
About Joy	56
To Procrastination	60
On Taking Action	64
To (Imp)atience	68
To Share Serenity	72
On Rainy-Day Boredom	75
To Create Curiosity	78
To Deal With Doubt	81
To Embrace Hope	85
About Stress and Overwhelm	89
On Surrender	95

To Pain	98
On For-Giveness	103
To Process Shame and Blame	110
On Acceptance and Responsibility	117
From Guilt	122
About Innocence and Redemption	126
To Fear	131
On Love	134
Afterword: Resources	137
About the Author	145

Preface

Dear Extraordinary and Blessed Reader,

I am most human. I make mistakes, do not always speak in the most loving ways, or say what I mean—especially in the heat of the moment. However, I love writing letters! They provide Divine inspiration and afford me the time I need to formulate my ideas and share what is in my heart. The end result is then something measured, clear, tangible, and loving.

As a young teen, I wrote my first *official* Love letter to my godparents, Jim and Mary Fuerth (RIP), who lived a few hours away from me. I poured out my heart, expressing gratitude for their kindness and support. My godfather told me years later that he was so moved by my letter that he kept it in his wallet to re-read.

Then, as an older teenager in the early 1980s, I attended Catholic high school retreats called COR (Christ in Others Retreat). Part of that weekend involved a couple of letter-writing exercises. We wrote to our parents first, sharing how much we appreciated and loved them. Right after that exercise, we were then directed to write a message of Love to ourselves, acknowledging and celebrating our positive qualities. Retreat facilitators gathered up all of the letters.

Unbeknownst to us, the letters to our parents were distributed to them while they waited to surprise us at the close of the weekend. During the retreat, we also received correspondence from family, friends, COR peers, and especially our parents, which shared their blessings and Love. Needless to say, when teenagers saw their loved ones at the end of the retreat, tears flowed freely and the seeds for better relationships took root.

About two weeks after my return home, I received my self-written Love letter in the mail. I can still remember sitting on my bed, eagerly opening up and drinking in those encouraging words and paying that forward in enthusiastically scripted Love letters to my new COR friends.

As a result of the pain in my marriage and its subsequent ending, I could no longer remain with the church of my childhood. But I am forever grateful for the COR experience and those life-changing activities.

My boys were ages 6, 4, and 1 when I separated in 1993. All of the financial, emotional, spiritual, practical, and physical challenges that I faced as a low-income, sole support parent prompted me to reach out for and find support through counselling, workshops, retreats, courses, and books.

Without having an open mind and learning new ways of being a healthier parent, my children would only acquire the child-rearing patterns that their dad and I had learned. Bearing almost all of the parental responsibility also stretched my Love muscle and I was deeply committed to raising my children well and to the best of my ability.

My sons have taught me so much about the exponential nature of Love. Together as a family, we have travelled across the messy terrain of feelings and experienced the trials and triumphs of living in a single parent household. These amazing, talented, bright, and loving souls have been my biggest motivators and have helped me become a better person.

Love Letters

During that first year of separation, I attended a much-needed women's retreat. While there, I was introduced to a letter-writing exercise that etched itself into my heart. In it, I met my older and wiser Self. In the first letter, I directed questions *to* this Wise One, who had already lived through all of my challenges at that time.

A reply letter *from* my Wise One answered my questions and, with a message of loving care and support, helped put my circumstances and feelings into perspective. Guiding me to choices and experiences that would create more positive outcomes, my older, wiser Self had already successfully managed everything in my life at that time and could navigate me through the rough spots.

That letter-writing exercise transformed me, as I communicated heart-to-heart with that Divine inner knowing: the intuitive, all-loving, connected Self—my God-Self—with unlimited wisdom and Love coming through to help. My Wise One never blamed, shamed, judged, or berated me for my feelings or my choices at the time. Instead, I was always reminded how much I was loved, how much I loved my children, and how I could view my circumstances differently. I felt ever more optimistic and trusting that life would improve. And it did.

For a few years, I designed and delivered journal-writing workshops for the general public and various groups, incorporating these letter-writing exercises. I always felt blessed to witness the authentic and *warm fuzzy* feelings that participants shared during the time we spent together. Their inner Wise Ones showed up to help them, too!

I communicated daily with my Wise One while attending and completing university, as I explored various healing modalities, and when I began working with low-income individuals in a Social Services setting. Creativity, positivity, and serendipity increased. I processed feelings in more effective ways, becoming a better mom and person. Far from God-like, I accepted that I was perfectly imperfect…as we all are.

My heightened spiritual experience as a teenager and this reconnection to my Wise One evolved into a way of thinking, feeling, and creative writing that helped produce the following letters. However, I cannot claim full ownership of them, for they are messages that came *through* me from the Divine.

Love Letters

The following passage in my journal (written at a healing workshop facilitated by Dr. Adam McLeod in 2013) aptly captures a Truth that could apply to all of us:

We are more than just our bodies. We are loved beyond measure. Yet, how can we measure Love? What quantifies it? Who can calibrate it? Nothing and no one. Except that in its presence, all colour sparkles and deepens. All hearts re-member. All resistance ceases.

If I were to keep what is in my heart yet give voice to that which seeks expression, the two would not be mutually exclusive.

*Isn't what we are called to do here **the** most important function of Life?*
If not now...when?
If not here...where?
If not me...who?
If not with Love...how?

These Love letters offer us new ways of understanding, when we accept all of our feelings that arrive, sometimes unannounced, in our hearts and everyday lives.

Extraordinary Loving for Everyday Living

Written with a philosopher's mind, a poet's eye, and a lovin'-u-large soul, various styles of writing are embodied in these letters: from prose, to metaphor, to poetry. Just as we are not one-dimensional, neither would be my writing and your reading.

I have taken poetic license with the spelling and capitalization of some words, to more easily expose their deeper meanings and significance. The noun *Love* is also capitalized and sprinkled liberally throughout this book, because we could all use more Love! These are not proof-reading errors but an intentional and creative use of the English language.

What do I do with a Love letter after I have written it? I usually send it. When I am having fun I *want* to share it. But when I see how much suffering is going on in our world, I *need* to share it.

This is the first in a series of Love letters books. Know that I am deeply grateful for the gift of your time. May you access your own Divine Wise One and practice extraordinary loving in your everyday living!

Sharing Love,
Paulette Dahl

Acknowledgments

Dear Uber-Talented People and Loved Ones:

Books do not just magically appear. They are created. Not just *by* the writer, but *through* the writer, by everyone who has contributed to that writer being able to write and have what was written make sense. This book has been wondrously and miraculously made.

I launched an Indiegogo campaign on September 16, 2014 to assist me with the cost of producing and publishing this book and two days later, a co-worker suddenly died. Two days after that, my dad passed away and the campaign's momentum faltered. However, without the help of the following generous souls, this book would still be sitting in a file on my computer. Words cannot express my heart-felt gratitude for the incredible gift of *you*!

Love Letters

Profound Love 'n' Gratitude go to the following contributors:

Amanda Lowen Hill	Steve Lowen
Cindy Doering	Christine Schrum
Pam Jackson	Wayne Gauthier
Louise Visneskie	Joanne Kaattari
Elaine Faris	Susan Little
Benton McLean	Anthony Gras
Christopher Gras	Gregory Gras
John Howley	Ron Menard
Jeanine Middleton	Britney St. Pierre
Rhya Repele	Cathy Mete Ali
Nick Zelinger	Ronnie Moore

I am also deeply grateful for the professionals I have met, who have helped me in so many ways.

Please refer to the Afterword for their contact information. I cannot think of a better way to begin and end these Love letters than by spreading the word about their essential skills, support, and positive influence.

I am honoured to be assisted by the talent of the following people, who helped get my ideas into book

Extraordinary Loving for Everyday Living

form: Dr. Judith Briles (AuthorU Extravaganza/The Book Shepherd), Joel Friedlander (building a platform and first steps coach), Nick Zelinger (book cover design), Ronnie Moore (interior book design and book layout), Laura E. Young (first editor), Kimberly Fahner (second editor), Wayne Gauthier (editor/feedback), Joanne Kaattari (promotion/feedback), Christine Schrum (feedback), Greg Tremblay (videographer for the Indiegogo campaign), and Beatriz Tejeiro (crowdfunding).

The following provide healing of mind, body, and/or spirit and are all helping make the world a better place—one person at a time: Ron Menard (Heal Inc.), Dr. Greg Baer (Real Love™ books, program, and retreats), Klaus Buentemeyer (Green Bay Lodge retreat and healing sessions), Marsha and Crystal Best (Acupuncturist-Traditional Chinese Medicine and Magneto Therapy), Dr. Adam McLeod, Naturopath (and Dreamhealer books/videos), and Dr. Bradley Nelson (*The Emotion Code* and *The Body Code™ Program* author).

My birth family influenced me in many ways while I was growing up. I appreciate what I have learned from

Love Letters

Walter and Theresa Dahl—my parents (RIP), and wish all of my siblings peace, Love, and healing.

Without the ongoing support, guidance, encouragement, acceptance, and Love from *framily* (friends who are closer than family), my sons, my creativity, and I would not have found such a nurturing place to grow.

Joanne Kaattari is one of the most encouraging and action-oriented framily members, having invited me over 20 years ago to attend a Freelance Writing Workshop with her. I cherish the feel-good memory of us writing out our hearts and sharing our hopes and dreams. She, her husband Steve Wells, and children Nick Bainard and Evan Wells are all big-hearted and Love-filled people!

Steve Lowen is another framily member who came into our lives in 1995 as a volunteer with the Big Brothers organization when he was matched with my eldest son. He has extended kindness, support, generosity, and welcome to my family and me. Love keeps getting bigger and bigger! We are blessed to be part of his family, along with his loving and encouraging wife, Amanda, and their beautiful and spirited children, Eleanore and Clark!

Other dearly loved framily members who know all about me (and love me anyway) include: Cindy Doering, Karen Krushelnick, Diana Fernandez, Maureen & Jules Lapierre, Wayne Gauthier, Louise, Brian & Sarah Visneskie, Mary Lou Fabbro & Hadyn Butler, Caterina Mete-Ali, Elaine Faris, Deb Pindur, Ron Menard, and Christine Schrum. I am extremely grateful for their heart-full kinship and for helping me be a better person and writer!

Bright lights include: Mindie Mullen & Tony Hacquard, Sylvie Taylor, Leslie & Tom Middleton, Pam Jackson, Valerie Senyk, Eveline Boyd, Lee-Ann Turja, Caroline Pawluk & David Schrum, Christiane Corriveau, Pat Morgan, Stephen Heiti, Melanie Martilla, Darryl Mazzuchin, Susan Little, Karen Thistle, Lisa Brown-Coleman, and Leah Fryer Niwranski. They share their creativity and blessings with the world!

My co-workers in Social Services are some of the most generous, supportive, and helpful people I know! Forgive me for not naming everyone, but with almost

100 people in that division, there are too many names to mention. However, I am especially thankful for my Manager, Vivienne Martin, and colleagues in Employment Support Services (past and present): Rick Carriere, Carmen Depatie, Deanna Dumas, Helen Landry, Amanda Leblanc, Pam Miller, Michelle Murphy-Castonguay, Rachel Noel de Tilly, Angela Paris, Tracy Peura, Renee Piette, Kathy Roberge, Jeanne Savard, and TinaWhitman. As well, I deeply appreciate all my 7th floor buddies! Everyone on our floor shares respect, camaraderie, food, and a welcoming attitude, which makes it so easy to come into work every day!

Former Writing Circle and Rectangle members hold a special place in my heart. In a confidential and creative space, we nurtured and challenged each other to hone our writing skills. They are talented writers who sparked my creativity, helped me forge on, and have shared some wonderfully spontaneous and uncensored writing. I also enjoy celebrating their Love of the written word by attending their book launches or theatre events!

If I have missed anyone, it is an omission on my part for which I apologize in advance. Just know how much I value and appreciate everyone who has touched my life!

Lovin'-U-Large,
Paulette

Introduction

Communicating with each other through the written word makes us distinctly human. Each letter has a unique shape and significance. When we put letters together they form a word and each word has meaning. Place words together and they can create a sentence, filled with text, subtext, and purpose. Individual letters, when combined, represent something much bigger than themselves. So it is with these Love letters. They are layered and complex, just like us. As a thoughtful form of communication, these written messages begin and maintain a committed dialogue between the sender and the recipient.

Unfortunately, letter-writing is at risk of becoming extinct. From tweets of 140 characters or less to text messages that abbreviate our language, we are hard-pressed to write or read any letters...let alone Love letters.

Yet, contained within this *toolbook* is a miraculous opportunity to experience something that may be outside of most people's comfort zone: *the feeling life.*

Love Letters

Our emotions represent an inner language which can be outwardly expressed or unfortunately remain repressed. They are important markers of our lives, helping us know when we are off-track and when we are completely in tune with our Selves, our loved ones, our environment, and the world. Feelings never end. They are as sure as each breath we inhale and exhale. They can overwhelm us, but we do not have to let them keep us in their grip indefinitely.

If you look at babies and young toddlers, before they have a chance to be molded into well-behaved little boys and girls, you will see how quickly they are able to process their emotions. They can be angry, sad, fearful, and joyful—all within minutes.

When all of their feelings flow through them and are not shut down, these young ones are at their most natural, connected, and content. They have something to teach us. If we allow what we feel to move through us, we can also be the most authentic, clear, connected, and at peace.

It is important to remember that it is not healthy to express our sentiments in an unkind or abusive way. In fact, doing so creates shame and takes us away from healing and making positive changes. It is most helpful if we feel safe, accepted, and loved while feelings are released. We become stronger, healthier, and more loving individuals and much more accepting of others who are going through their own process.

Underpinning all of our emotions is Love, even when we do not recognize that it is there. Love takes our human experience and makes it extraordinary by reminding us how absolutely connected we are to everything else. It is the foundational heart-space from which all things heal and grow. In the midst of our darkness, it shines as a beacon which draws us back to our Selves.

This book beckons us to access some of the most painful and also transcendent feelings. How often do we voluntarily source those *bring-you-down* emotions or their equalizing *lift-you-up* ones? While there may be a letter from depression, following it is also a balancing one about resilience. Reading about the grumpies is not complete without exploring gratitude.

We discover ways to discern and manage expressions like anger, grief, procrastination, loneliness, or fear. We can also learn how to see them differently and invite them to the banquet of our lives. If we ignore them, they loom larger-than-life and wreak havoc on our decisions, loved ones, and peace of mind. Let us not forget about those counter-balancing and welcome feelings, such as peace, joy, taking action, about belonging, or Love. When we take the time to recognize their positive influence, we are empowered to heal, grow, and lead by example.

We get so caught up in a world that appears to be divided: from countries, political parties, and religions, to families, and relationships. The theme played out is *I am right,* and *you are wrong.* It is so easy to look at our differences and see others as vastly separate from ourselves. Let us, however, put aside that erroneous disconnect and reconnect with what we share in common: our emotions, our humanness, and our most intimate God-Selves.

Love, in its subtle and not-so-subtle ways, frames and soothes our feelings. Let us embrace what so readily seeks to uplift and join: minds, hearts, bodies, and souls. This sublime energy calls forth a connection of such certainty that we all re-member who we are, why we are here, and how we can help each other be and bring out our best!

When we open up to this inner language of feelings, we can all benefit from this powerful liberation.

How To Use This Book

A tradesperson has a toolbox of tools at the ready to build again or anew. When we reach into this *toolbook*, we will find the appropriate material: insights, warmth, comfort, inspiring messages, and especially Love, to help us build again or anew.

This *toolbook* can be especially useful if you think of a circumstance or unresolved feeling that is on your mind or in your heart. Then, randomly open it up and read the letter on which you land. Please remember to also read the letter that is paired with the one you chose.

Another way that you can use this book is by looking at the Contents section at the front. If you see an emotion that you would like to explore more deeply, turn to that letter. Do not forget to read that letter's corresponding emotion.

These letters are deliberately paired to demonstrate the balancing aspects of life. No matter how you use this book, do not be surprised if what you read is perfectly positioned to comfort, inform, uplift, help, and love you.

I am a certified Life Coach (owner of Lovin'-U-Large Life Coaching), which I use with my intuitive Self in order to support others to be their best Selves.

For more in-depth self-discovery and to bring ideas into action, a companion *Extraordinary Loving for Everyday Living Work & Play Book* will be published at a future date, which includes questions and activities on each Love letter.

If you would like coaching or to participate in an experiential event, like a workshop or retreat using the Love letters material, or if you wish to provide feedback, please contact me at: *lovelettersbookspdahl@gmail.com*.

I look forward to hearing from you and doing my part to help bring forward healed hearts and transformation!

Love Letters

From Loneliness

Dear Ones Who Feel So Alone,

It has been awhile since I have caught your notice. While I have your attention, there are some things I wish to share:

- ♥ It is not necessary to distract...for that is worse than just acknowledging that I am here.
- ♥ I know how challenging it is to be away from the Divine, who could hold you so lovingly and close.
- ♥ It may not feel that way right now, but you are in a time of miraculous change, for you are open to learning important information.

What would happen, dear one, if you sat with me awhile? Would you cry? Would you reflect? Would you feel the emptiness of the space between your breaths? Would the quiet be deafening? Would you share some Love with this old, familiar friend—you know—the one you dread to see, for the Truth that always arrives with the visit? That underneath all of the activities you use to avoid, you are still faced with your life: the choices you have made, and the losses and gains you have experienced.

I want you to close your eyes and sit in the silence. Just *be* with me. There is no need for hurried activity or diversions. I promise not to overstay my welcome.

> You will find, as you embrace me, that you do not have to fear me.
> As you lose your fear of me, you will be more honest.
> As your Truth releases you, you will experience a new-found Passion.
> As your Passion settles into your Soul, you will feel Free.
> As your Freedom soars, so will your Joy.
> As your Joy abounds, so will Love come into fullness.

As Love comes into fullness, you will experience
   Grace.
As your Grace flows, so will Compassion.
And with Compassion, you will gather a choir of
   souls who seek to share their longing for Home.
And in that sharing is Communion.

Residing with All That Is, embracing each undivided being, you will discover that you have never truly been alone; instead, you have been truly asleep to that which nestles against and within you.

Do not be afraid to sit quietly in my presence, for it is there that you discover how deeply you are connected to all others and to Love. Love and connection are always and only a thought, a sigh, a breath, a tear, or a smile away. And it has no end. I look forward to meeting you again between your thoughts.

Love,
Loneliness

About Belonging

Dear Ones Who Seek Inclusion,

    It is no surprise that you feel a sense of disconnection, with the media blitzing dog-eat-dog news, reality shows demonstrating one-upmanship, and politics that engender an *us* versus *them* attitude. There are family members who ostracize other members, social media sites that allow one to unfriend or delete another at a click of a button. Lastly, our intimate relationships become battlegrounds with winners and losers, and Love appears nowhere to be found.

    In this world bent on instant gratification and impatience with long-term efforts for success, everyone is challenged to find the deeply residing heart that feels at Home.

    So many can find a place to live, but how many can be truly alive...to be fully alive in the Truth of that connection, with complete acceptance?

Isn't that the deeper question?

Be-longing is the longing to *be*, to understand who, why, where, how, and what you are and to be included with each other in that process of discovery and recovery.

No matter where you go, you take your Selves with you. You are faced, each moment, with being okay with who you are. Do you like being in your own skin?

Miracles occur in the enlightened mind, which collaborates with the resident heart and connects to the Divine soul. That bond expands into every root, branch, leaf, tributary, mountain, into the fertile soul and the expanse of sky, into the very particles of you and I. Understand how beautifully and wondrously we are all made!

Do you believe that not only are you the outcome of your errors, but also the combination of your gifts and talents?

If you were to honour the Love within that seeks to be expressed if it only felt safe enough, would you so readily armour yourselves and live behind walls of defense, or mount an attack?

Science has been able to prove that our basic molecular structure of carbon, oxygen, hydrogen, and nitrogen are also core elements that make up the Universe.

Even if you wanted to, you could not be separate from everything else, by virtue of your material make-up. We are that closely connected.

When this knowledge sifts deeply into you, allow the peace of that Truth to wash over and around you. Imagine a web, with intricate lines drawn between you and everything else. Notice that you are an intrinsic part of that network. Without you, there would be a broken link. You are that important. *You* matter.

Change starts with each one of us deciding to accept that we all belong: within our Selves, with each other, and with the world.

Our world depends on our re-member-ing that. We can achieve peaceful co-existence if we rise above the 'herd mentality' that seeks power by fostering fearful beliefs and outdated ways of being and relating.

What are we waiting for? Let us take just one small step in a different direction.

Extraordinary Loving for Everyday Living

When we offer a smile or a word of welcome to someone new, we demonstrate a more inclusive manner and create positive change. Let that expansive mind-set transform be-longing into belong-ing.

Loving you back to wholeness,
Love

To Avoid Confusion

Dear Perplexed Souls,

We live in a world that celebrates contradiction. There are so many ways that we are conditioned to create dramas and a sense of utter confusion. We ingest material that scrambles our bodies. We watch entertainment drivel or play mind-numbing games. Our souls are steeled against the next big scandal of lies: corporate greed and cover-ups by entrusted officials, clergy, or heads of companies.

We get distracted in thousands of ways as if running from our Truth will make life less boring. Or painful. Or hard.

What would happen if we sat down in the quietude of our space and allowed our Selves airplay? What kind of clarity would gently (or not-so-gently) find its way into our hearts?

Would it not be helpful to have clarity knowing where we belong, how to live without destroying our environment or each other, with whom to live, what feeds our souls, acknowledging that we have shortcomings, and how to address them? Let us discover the forgiveness within, share the Love we feel, do the correct thing, and live our complete purpose in joy.

Would that not be wondrous indeed? Would that not generate such energy, passion, and satisfaction that we would find few faults with ourselves, all of those around us, and in our world? Would that not create a groundswell of sated souls who would then be willing to share their clarity and direction with each other?

What if, in our stance of Love, we looked each other ever-so-kindly and gently in the eyes, sharing the strength of our certitude?

What if we accepted differences as part of a colourful, cultural mosaic, and made a conscious decision to get along so that we could offer peace rather than demands and joy instead of judgment?

When we watch children in their unbridled enthusiasm, we easily notice their obvious delight. Their willingness to accept differences and embrace the moment demonstrates gifts that we do not readily acknowledge. Their willingness to ask questions and be open to answers are attitudes from which we adults could learn. And grow. And begin anew.

So, instead of fortifying rigid walls of defensiveness, if we remain open to new information and ways of seeing, we reduce confusion. Similarly, if we are too muddled and unable to concentrate, if we remember one step that has helped us get clear in the past and use it this time, we can get very focused on what works for us.

Avoiding confusion by asking for clarity is the loving step to take. And listening to the answers will garner new peace of mind, either immediately or eventually.

When we drop down into our hearts, using our intuition and truly listening to what someone is telling us, we can hear the Truth. Confusion occurs most easily when we do not accept someone else's or our own Truth, and our expectations are not met.

Confusion, then, is really a red herring that takes us away from asking the right questions that would give us the definite (although not always welcome) answers we seek. Confusion is another distracting tool we use to avoid the pain of rejection, separation, or loss.

Yet no matter what happens, we are loved: both in confusion and in clarity. It is just that we do not need to suffer unnecessarily.

Each moment...we can begin anew...in the clearness of each moment of distinction.

Trusting in your decision-making process.

Love,
Love

About Clarity

Dear Clear and Confident Souls,

Think about a time when you knew exactly what you wanted and how to go about getting it. Remember how sure and confident you felt?

These feelings inspire us to share our enthusiasmos (Greek term for *God within*) with others. That energy is infectious and also attractive to those who are excited to support, or in some way help, us to achieve our goals.

With laser-like focus, we set out our steps and celebrate as each one is met. Sometimes, those steps are taken quite deliberately, and other times, they are taken through the nebulous process termed serendipity—the faculty of making fortunate discoveries by accident.

When we are clear about the direction in which we want to go, we set in motion all of the pieces and players that can contribute to a successful destination.

The more willing we are to be open to asking questions and learning new things, the more easily events tend to flow in our favour.

If we know we are going downstream, for example, then we can get in the canoe with our supplies and paddle with strong, confident strokes.

It is when we resist and second-guess our course that we struggle so frantically. What other strategies can we use to help us meet our end goal? One strategy we could try is the following: When we can *see* ourselves doing what we strive for, and *feel* the gratitude and confidence surging within us, we are creating an environment of discernment and commitment.

That feeling-state then creates the most amazing energy. We don't just *feel* like some sort of super-hero in our lives; we *are* a super-hero.

We tackle our bad guy thinking and behaviours with absolute precision and commitment. We slay our own internal dragons, bent on draggin' us down to mediocrity and low-level living.

Each dream that is part of our purpose and that we keep alive and work on, each small step in front of the other, are affirmations of our doingness.

Love Letters

We continue to shine. Like the sun behind the cloud cover, we are not dimmed by the occasional grey blanket day.

We do not spend much time wallowing in self-pity or indecision. We look for the solution and move full steam ahead.

Confidence is sexy. When it oozes out of our pores, we shimmer and glow with a luminescence that beckons others to also shine. When we are filled to the brim with our passion, we inspire others to grab their gusto, too.

We do not need to waste time on those who seek to keep us small and fearful. We thank them for what they show us and wish them luck on their journey.

We do not need to lose sleep over endings, either. We can just embrace the lesson, the Love, and let go of the feelings of despair.

When we are invested in our own dreams, we do not support living any nightmares. That is relegated to night-time dreaming, not to conscious living in the light of day.

Let us embrace our grandest visions. Let us honour our hero or heroine's path. Let us also support others in their grandest visions and together we will experience even more luminosity in Life and Love.

Loving the true and confident you,
Love

About the Grumpies

Dear Fellow Grumps,

> Do you ever allow yourself to admit that you feel grumpy?
> Have you ever noticed how easy it is to slip into *poor me* thinking?

Watch what happens next:

- Powerlessness sets in.
- Feelings get amplified.
- Everything around you responds to that subtle (and not so subtle) soul-sucking energy.
- Then more of the same experiences hammer at the door.
- Grumpy becomes a way of life.

Do you ever feel grumpy about how hard you have worked and how little it feels you have to show for it? Sometimes, aren't you just plain tired that things haven't changed? And do you ever feel grumpy with yourself because you feel you should believe that your life is changing? Don't you feel that you should know better than surrendering to this feeling of lack or you should know what happens when you start comparing yourself to others? Don't you find that as soon as you *should* yourself, you *shit* on yourself? Have you ever felt grumpy about feeling grumpy and then beaten yourself up with *shoulds*? That is like a double-whammy grump!

Power-brokers play a role in this world that confuses financial prowess with prestige, entitlement, material possessions, status, and *being somebody*. You are treated like you are not a zero as long as you have a bunch of zeroes after a number in your bank account. How mixed-up is that? Who you are is not defined by how much money or possessions you have.

What happened to Love? It is during times like these when it helps if you accept that you feel what you are feeling. Then make a decision to stop being so hard on yourself. Ask the Divine to help you feel less tired of not measuring up to such a limited standard of living, which is woefully inadequate to handle the stress that most of us wear so regularly. Money cannot buy the intangibles like faith, optimism, gratitude, or Love. It is a means of exchange and an outward reflection of an inner belief. Reaching out to others, not to compare but to commiserate, can help lessen our burdens.

While you may want and even say you *love* something, *things* cannot love you back. People can love you. You can love you. Most importantly: your Divine Self always loves you. And that Love has no strings attached. There is no fine print voiding the warranty of Love.

Hope springs eternal. Faith in something greater than yourself imbues your spirit. Abundance on all levels reminds you that you cannot do more with less. You can do so much more with more: wealth, health, Love, joy, peace, forgiveness, compassion, authenticity, strength, and especially, thankfulness.

Gratitude gains back your dignity. Gratitude is an incredible antidote for the grumpies and it usually helps downgrade grumpy to just a *grr*...and then *g*...as in Gee! Time to release some more things for healing.

Love fuels us to grow past the grumpies. And the best part of getting past the grumpies? Sharing! One of the best gifts of Life is sharing. Especially Love. When it pours out of us...because grumpies cannot stay fixed in the forever of Love!

Cheers to a freer you,
Love

With Gratitude

Greetings in Appreciation,

   Love, we go hand-in-hand. I arrive when you are acknowledged, as the warmth that settles in hearts after a blessed event.
   When someone shares you, Love, their ability to offer thanksgiving is amplified and they glow with great full-ness (or gratefulness).
   It is our inherent play-fullness that also inspires those to call us forth. Love 'n' Gratitude. Gratitude 'n' Love. The power team that creates miraculous transformation, makes things happen, enters into the stillness and silliness, caresses in lovers' looks, embraces in the deepest connections, puts smiles on empty faces and longing hearts, raises eyes and hands in praise, and belts out songs of joy!
   Where would I be without you? You make living extra alive, as an agent for all that can be celebrated and

recognized. Even in the midst of intense pain or sadness, when we are summoned there is a sense of relief and a feeling of peace also descends.

We are a forever force that builds up energy and optimism, challenges and supports, excites those around us to herald Love 'n' Gratitude from deep within their souls. The light emanates from their bodies, which shines on even the darkest thoughts, dispelling the shadows.

All is revealed when we come to the rescue, for we make certain that the Truth is cradled in our tender care. Never thinking or saying a mean word, we mean every word we say. There is *always* someone to love. There is *always* something for which to be grateful. There is *always* the opportunity to share the sweetness of Life through Love 'n' Gratitude.

It does not only happen when others *deserve* it either. Lives are forever changed when it is shared during times of conflict and pain. For it is truly amazing to offer someone better treatment than what they feel they deserve. Think how transformed is the behaviour of one who is loved and appreciated, especially when they have not *earned* it.

Truly, seeing beyond the personality (and all of its human foibles) forges a connection that witnesses to the Divine within.

Our team is not whole, one without the other. We are so much more when we are invited to honour life. And we always enjoy a good party!

We can range in our expression from quiet, meditative, restorative reflection to an all-out shout-from-the-rooftops public declaration of WOO-HOO!

Our flexibility is also second to none and our combined duo of dedication creates and re-creates.

We recommend people don a generous gown of Gratitude and slip on a comfortable mantle of Love the next time anyone is inclined to walk naked into a relationship, because these coverings will allow the unfolding of vulnerability to occur with the highest respect and honour.

We get things done! And we cause resentments and built-up walls of resistance to be undone.

This happens with each small step we take. Within each moment there is a sacred choice: to be grateful or to grumble. To love or lash out.

The choice is simple enough to see, yet takes courage and discipline to practice. People can be such creatures of habit. But just watch where we lead when we enthusiastically inch others forward!

With Gratitude,
with Love!

From Depression

Dear Ones Who Feel So Burdened,

Here I sit. Or lie. Or stare. I cannot seem to rouse this body to move. It takes every ounce I have to think. Much less feel. Or plan.

Pain can course throughout. It hurts. Sometimes, a lot. Other times, it is like a dull ache. I feel heavy. Like an anchor around the heart. Stone. Thick as stone. A wall that stops others from reaching me.

Shutting myself off from everyone else keeps me alone. With thoughts that do not cease. They are unrelenting. Not meant to release me. Keeping everything in.

Thoughts are disjointed in a foggy mind. Questions jump at me: *"What is the point? Who cares? Not again? Does it matter? Do I matter?"*

I cannot seem to escape these words, feelings, myself.

Energy is a rare commodity. Even the air around me seems dense and clogging. I walk as if wading through Jell-O. It prompts me to stop. Stopped. Blocked. The feelings of hopelessness cascade throughout me again. Where is the rainbow in that?

The only colour I see is grey. A monochromatic view from eyes that dare not see.

Everyone around me whispers. They care but do not know how to help. Those who have never plumbed these depths are cruel with their words: "Snap out of it. Stop feeling sorry for yourself. There are people worse off than you and you don't hear them complain. If you just did"—and they fill in the blanks—"you would feel better. Why aren't you taking medication?"

They all seem to think they are the experts on me. Like they know exactly what I need, without recognizing that they cannot live as me. What works for them only works for them, not necessarily for everyone else.

Others who have had me in their midst offer more compassion, understanding, and suggestions. They do not judge and around them I do not hide.

But spending time with people is exhausting. Time merges from one day to the next. One week into the other. A month into a year. A year into oblivion. And so it goes.

Low-level feelings simmer beneath a lid or it is a gloom that casts its long shadow. Looking through what seems like a dark tunnel, I see a pinprick of light in the far distance. I hear, "*Come here. You are so loved.*"

That light beckons me. It pierces me and anchors into my depths, pulling me towards it. "*You are so loved. You are so loved.*"

The journey through this tunnel is arduous. I am scared and yet, slowly, one small step at a time, I make my way closer and closer to the end of the tunnel. At first, I do not really believe that I am loved. I react in defense as if it were not true.

But the loving comments continue. I feel accepted and truly understood. There is no hurry and no expectation.

"Come closer. You are so loved. You can do it."

More and more light surrounds the opening. There are many ways of reaching me, for I am a hungry sort.

But underneath them all is the fundamental belief that I am loved. No matter how long I stay inside. No matter what I need. Hearing *"you are so loved"* becomes my mantra.

I begin to believe it. Really feel it. This warmth in my core begins to fill my emptiness.

The opening of light grows larger and features of those reaching for me start to take shape.

Colours vividly splash into view. An azure blue sky. White cotton ball clouds. Emerald green grass. Trees wave their leaves in welcome. Hands attached to arms attached to bodies open to receive me. Lips smile. Eyes lock.

I am aware and in awe of this born-again world: the sharp aroma of coffee and the subtle scents. Smooth and rough surfaces. The ground that stays solid beneath me.

I am so much more than any label on a piece of paper. I bring others to know themselves. Truly know themselves. For we all originate from Love.

"You are so loved." That is what I believe today. And I accept that the present is a gift and it is enough for now.

Love Letters

Do not fear me and do not shun me.
Please do not run and hide.
Do not disguise me or pretend I am not here.
All I ask is for you to use Love and let it be
    my guide.

Love,
Depression

About Resilience

Dear Strong Ones of Heart,

When times grow really challenging and all of your resources are tapped, it is helpful to remember that the more something is flexible, the less possibility it will break.

While the circumstances may be outside of your control, your attitude is absolutely within your power. And how powerful you are, indeed!

You decide if something bothers you. So while life may have taken a turn that bothers everything within you, with a steady mind and roll-with-the-punches outlook, you strengthen the outcome in your favour.

There are those rare souls for whom life has been nothing but charmed. They lacked no creature comforts, everyone around them loved them, experiences unfolded seamlessly, and everything they touched was blessed.

However, what would happen to them if a circumstance occurred beyond their control?

Adversity creates growth because it is during the toughest times that someone discovers how tough they are. Not in-your-face-screw-you tough. But steely determined, persistent, and take-a-deep-breath-keep-going tough.

What does it mean to be that strong and resilient? It means facing something head-on. Addressing the issue rather than avoiding it. Clearing out the emotional debris. If something hurts, feel it. Then let it go. Whatever healthy process works for you, do that. If you have no process to handle the contrariness of life, then find those resources and supports that can provide options and things to try that you can adapt to suit you.

Then make each decision as a promise to yourself that you can handle whatever happens. Because you can.

Decide to make and honour a promise that you will emerge on the other side of rough waters. Your life raft will not sink. And neither will you.

Find the courage inside you that shores up your resolve. Going within helps you keep your equilibrium, as you can trust that you are your own best ally.

Believing in something much greater than yourself also provides an even stronger support, as that places you in a position of power, because you know that you are connected to every other being. This guarantees that you are never alone.

Resilience is like a perennial plant. The winter may appear to deaden the ground, but as soon as the ground warms, each spring, a shoot arises that reminds you that the plant was lying dormant, just waiting to burst into life.

It is in the ending of something that seeds are sown for something new.

Just as Nature expresses its cycle of birth, death, rebirth, so do you move through cycles. Busy time, then rest. Building, then nesting. Sowing, then reaping.

With others, then alone. Always an ebb and flow which is never intended to leave you high and dry, or flooded and cast adrift.

Love is the recognition that you are going to be okay, no matter what goes on around you. Change takes commitment, but Love requires belief.

Love Letters

There is no room for unrealistic expectation, which only sets you up for intense disappointment. Just accepting yourself and your circumstance helps you breathe a little easier. Breathing helps immeasurably. Take one deep breath in, a pause, then a deep breath out.

You've got this. You will emerge victorious, with so much more wisdom to share!

Love,
Your Faith-full Beloved

For Fatigue

Dear Weary Ones,

Droopy lids at half-mast, bleary eyes struggle to remain open. Yawns stretch for seconds into more seconds, in a naturally designed attempt to fill lungs and feed the brain with vital oxygen—life-breath that echoes within a tired body and a yearning soul. These are signs of shortened sleep and interrupted slumberous nights.

The body gives even more clues to your internal and external condition. The message is clear: there is a necessary repair and it is imperative to take the recuperative time to rest. Energy which keeps moving outwardly cannot be replenished. Each sleepless night unfolds into a dreary pattern of a watched clock ticking into twilight, creating compounded restlessness.

Bone-weary exhaustion causes a breach in relationships, for there is no time for others in an insurmountable schedule: a frenetic pace with no finish line and time is money, but money cannot buy more time. Seconds turn into minutes, that turn into hours, that run into days, which merge into weeks, that morph into months and chock up into years of a blurred existence, punctuated only by brief pauses, with diminishing effect.

Fatigue, you are the ever-present tiredness that lingers in edges alongside consciousness. Each successive, busy step brings you further away from the rest of You. Cumulative sleeplessness leads to a diminished life, with short tempers, frayed nerves, inattentive half-lives. Deciding that rest is not a selfish act but an act of Self-Love, gives you permission to halt and rejuvenate. And the greatest actions that speak louder than words are feeling loved, valued, and accepted.

Truly *feeling* it—not just as a mental exercise (although fake-it-until-you-make-it works), but also placing that Love in each cell, allowing it to wash over, around and in each system, so that you are gently relieved of your duty and the body can then be restored at all levels.

So, I offer you the blanket of my Love. Settle in and enjoy the warmth of relaxing into me: your Beloved, assuring that you are protected from everyday worries or deeper-seated angst, which prevents complete tranquility. Know that you are restored when you allow deep breaths to soothe molecules of activity, calming your state of high alert.

With a grateful heart and a guiltless rundown of the day's events, you can firmly relegate all activities and worries to the past. Then focus on succumbing to the gently quieting mind, so the body can slip into a state of being, where there is no need to do.

Thank you, for the gift of your presence.

Love,
Love

To Passion

Dear Energizer,

You are the conductor that fuels dreams into becoming reality. You boost sagging spirits with your *can-do* belief. You inspire creative works, changed hearts and a renewed zest for life. When someone embraces you, their enthusiasm becomes infectious, as they demonstrate and motivate others to discover and follow what sparks their imaginations and makes their souls soar.

Your energy can manifest in something as simple as living in nature to something as grand as changing the human condition halfway across the world.

Nothing is too intimidating when people are seized by your enthusiasm and committed determination to follow along a path that fulfills their purpose. They look plugged in to your natural high and they can work long hours and still maintain a smile on their faces for they are connected to an unlimited well-spring, from which anything is possible.

Desire is part of your drive, as is the quiet yearning in contemplative hearts. Yours is the mo-jo that writes Love songs, courts conquests and resolutions, and blazes a trail of such conviction that others are inspired to follow their own inner calling. You do not take no for an answer and you always rebound after a set-back, with unfailing optimism and fervour. You are the backbone of devotion and a loyal servant of Truth.

What, then, makes you so elusive in our everyday lives? Why do we accept mediocrity and leave you beating restlessly in our breasts?

Perhaps there is a subtle (and not so subtle) message that we can never have our wishes fulfilled, for we are part of a consumerist society and then brainwashed into never being content enough with material things.

That is when Love causes us to seek further than the acquisition of trinkets and we challenge ourselves to sign up for that course, write that book, approach that stranger, believe in the impossible, take that risk into the unknown, and follow where it may lead.

Love Letters

You bob along waves of desire, buoyed by the strength of your bonds, a yearning that stirs deep within minds and bodies. Love is the eternal bliss upon which you ride.

Passion, you are not just for lovers, you are for those who choose to satisfy their desire to live a purposeful life. And your energy has no end, as each ripple morphs into ever-expanding waves that influence everyone in their wake. You bring joy into exchanges and transform the mundane into the miraculous. Imagine what happens when someone celebrates Love in action. It is magical, mystical, and magnificent.

In the world of possibility exists all latent probability, which succeeds into distinct opportunity through persistence, work, will, serendipity, and Love. Thank you, Passion, for your boundless and limitless energy and fun!

Love,
Love

About Anger

Dear Seething Souls,

We can get so royally riled up when our expectations of others are unmet. We set ourselves up for conflict and disconnection, all of which are felt in our bodies when our jaws clench, our necks tense, and our stomachs start to burn. Chemicals are released that fuel our flight-or-fight response. Usually, the fight wins as we hurl words like emotional ballistic missiles, targeting those in the present who have triggered pain from our past, and who may feel that we are the unwitting victims of someone else's behaviour.

And we can erupt, either with a tirade of seething syllables or in a withdrawn, hostile retreat, creating both ends of a spectrum of disrespect in which nobody wins. This is the embodiment of disconnection. Anger does not serve in this way—it severs.

Yes, anger is the fuel that propels us to make a change. However, rage that is fuelled for a long time can turn into a burning resentment and hatred, which gnaws at us, causing dis-ease and preventing peace of mind. Hatred is a strong word, but anger is a strong emotion that can perpetuate itself and has created generational feuds, domestic violence, and war.

If we are tired of the same outcomes, taming that initial irritation can help us choose a different approach, response, path, or partner. The operative word is *different*.

No longer accepting behaviour or treatment that is not healthy or supportive, we can share our annoyance without the need for over-kill. We are relieved when we get things off our chests and share our needs, as long as we can be respectful.

We need to ask ourselves and others why we feel mad, being as specific as possible. Looking underneath the issue, like seeing a snake under the rock, we will come face-to-face with the source of our temper. Usually, we are not just piqued about the current circumstance and for the reason we think. Often, below the anger is an unmet feeling or need, like vulnerability or grief or unresolved abuse, or attachment to an outcome that does not allow another person the freedom to choose as they wish.

We can be angry about how we opened ourselves to another without knowing if they were capable of mature relating. We can feel past rejections and hurt, or a deep disappointment in ourselves for *knowing* something was not going to unfold as we wanted, yet we charged into it anyway.

Or we are legitimately feeling that how we are currently being treated is unfair, unkind, hurtful, and unnecessary and we are no longer accepting that disrespectful treatment.

So what do we do with this heated emotion when it signals its arrival? Can we first own the idea that we are upset: bitter, resentful, enraged, or even filled with hate? Acknowledging that takes some of the intensity out of its power.

Feel the anger. Let it work its way through, rather than staying stuck—especially in the neck, shoulders, stomach, and muscles. Some people require a physical release, like a brisk walk or run, kick-boxing, swimming, squash, or any other activity that helps blow off steam.

Love Letters

But we need to remember that no one is obligated to alleviate our suffering. It is not always one hundred percent someone else's fault, either.

It is *always* one hundred percent our responsibility to handle what anger is telling us, so it can stimulate us to take action. Many times, through sourcing and processing our fury, we re-solve to do something differently, or we make a definite decision.

We also decide whether we need to tell whomever we may be angry with that we are peeved. Or we may be quite okay to process that feeling and only then share what we decided and how we will prevent that occurrence again.

The spiritually mature individual does not easily grow irate. Or much at all. But it is also not spiritually mature to pretend that we are not angry when we actually are. Authenticity is key.

There are some people whose default setting is immediate irritation and everyone else is *at fault*. They see the world as adversarial and are, unfortunately, easily connected to a seething volcano beneath the surface, waiting to burst.

There are others who do not wish to identify with their anger, but it still emerges as passive-aggressiveness or subtle forms of belittling or bullying, usually in the guise of wanting to help someone see where they are wrong.

Still others use sarcasm, which has a double whammy effect, since they are attacking another through the use of humour, and, if the other does not laugh, then that person is seen as being too sensitive or not able to take a joke.

And, unfortunately, there are others who absolutely refuse to acknowledge and appropriately process their anger and they have chronic illness or other health-related issues.

Where is Love in all of this? Well, Love is the antidote to anger, soothing the surge and bringing us back to a place of peace. Love helps us find the words and the intention to heal a conflict, not proliferate it. Love gives us the hope to believe that improvement and change are possible. Love gives us permission to express our anger in healthy ways and without having to find a scapegoat on which we dump our emotions.

Anger certainly has no healthy benefit stuck in our bodies, minds, or spirits. Love sets us free and, through that release, we are able to have an elevated perspective. Love helps us see the bigger picture in the dramas of our lives, not getting too caught up in the details but focusing more closely on what lesson can be learned.

We can always rely on loving thoughts and actions to bring us back from a spiteful episode, to help us bridge our differences, and to create renewed energy towards making things work or detaching with dignity. Love is the key ingredient to problem-solving after the huffing and puffing have dissipated. Love is the glue that pieces together peaceful dialogue.

Let us always be mindful that we are not only our anger and that it does not have to control us. Yet, when we give it the respect it deserves, miracles can occur. Let us find our energy shifting from seething to soothing, always with peace of mind and homeostasis within the heart.

I remain yours,
Love

To Inspire Peace

Dear Peaceful Souls,

How do you define peace?

Peace is obviously the absence of conflict. However, it can be hard-won—a deep sense of rightness, both within and without, that wraps itself around you like a cloak. Peace can feel like a natural flow of energy, allowing circumstances and people to be what and who they are without getting bogged down in how things unfold.

Masters of spiritual discipline regularly place themselves in the eye of the storm, observing more than involving themselves and reacting to others. A certain level of detachment to outcomes can promote greater peace.

It is unfair for anyone to dictate a path for peace... especially if that path creates conflict. As with any path that is first traveled, however, there are potential stumps, blockages, and unclear markers along the way.

If peace is an end result or destination, then the process may not be as important, as each challenge can bring you closer to an end point.

If peace is not only the end point, but the means to an end, then you will need to decide what is acceptable as the journey progresses. Be sure to acknowledge that which is upsetting you. Then surrender your upset in an appropriate way. Yelling, fighting, giving the silent treatment, putting up walls, being unkind, and hurtful are sure ways to feed anger, not relieve it.

Some individuals pursue the following activities or interactions that bring peace: meditating, walking in nature, listening to music, or sharing a loving conversation with a close friend or relative.

Others find solace in praying, singing, being with animals, writing, enjoying the natural high that comes from vigorous activity (physically releasing the pent-up discord), emptying the mind, reading, or watching inspirational movies.

There are those who enjoy thinking about the blessings that abound, being grateful, financial freedom, health, connected relationships, self-reflection, and awareness, being completely focused in the present, accepting people and circumstances, connecting to the Divine within, being creative, or sharing laughter.

Still others find serenity within any circumstance, unfazed by life's curves. These people most often draw others to them, as if being near someone at that level of peace can somehow be transferred. Most certainly, their calm influence acts as a balm for harried individuals, although these same serene souls may irritate Type A personalities who are driven to succeed. They may even view a calm attitude as a sign that someone may have a *laissez-faire* disposition, even if they do not.

There is really no limit to peace-making activities, especially when we have a questing spirit. Finding out what brings us peace can help towards creating more of it in our lives. Not knowing is an exciting place, as we can then explore new ways to experience peace.

Sadly, for some, peace will only occur when they die. Not familiar with the deep sense of contentment and stability that peace can offer, these individuals seek chaos, get easily annoyed, or unconsciously draw that to themselves so that their lament is one of wanting peace, but never doing what it takes to have it. Finding peace is a commitment to Love in action.

Sometimes, living in a place of peace requires us to be silent and take stock…reflect…listen to the still voice within us that knows and loves us so intimately and believes in our ability to determine the correct and best course of action in any given situation.

At other times, finding peace entails taking action to address a concern, state a need, voice a boundary, so that peace is the attained result.

At no time is peace ever out of reach. It is always available to those who seek it and always a constant to those who find themselves, more often than not, in a state of crisis.

Surrender to this feeling of peace as it envelops you in its loving, gentle embrace.

Love,
Love

To Grief

My Dear Grief,

When you arrive, you bring the piercing sharpness of a laser-like stab as breath is inhaled—a short, shallow breath, which cannot find enough oxygen to carry thoughts as they roam.

Holding back the eruption tightens the throat and jaw, causing a headache, only lessened by the heartache which cannot easily allow itself to release.

Full-out bore, the sobs escape, as a shower explodes from once-dry eyes. The tyranny of tears beat down upon the breast, the chest, with shaking hands that automatically stroke a contorting face.

Embrace that energy of surrender; go into it. Allow it to merge with you, so that you can feel its fullest effects and expulsion into the air, exclaiming your resistance that *this is not so*.

Love Letters

Oh, let me wrap you in my mantle,
as I hold you in my care.
But only after you've vented
the cruel injustice declaring "it's not fair."

Let me hold you in my comfort,
let me take all of you in.
Let me fearlessly lead you into the battle
of go away and go within.

With each levered air escaping
and each scream that is expelled,
with each convulsive movement,
I hug you close and ride the swell.

Self-contained but not containing,
self-aware but not too much,
full throttle on your engine,
but do not escape the clutch.

Extraordinary Loving for Everyday Living

Let me ease you into safety,
let my parachute power high,
let me bring you back from aloneness
and the depths of your decline.

Stay with this feeling that matters,
make your rhythm soft and strong,
know I can't ever abandon you,
for Love and grief forever belong.

With each fading sunset russet
riding out to greet the dawn,
I spark tiny shards of lightness
so that your soul can soldier on.

You are spent from all your tirades,
you are weathered from all of your ebbs.
I soft-whisper promises of healing
that dance into hearts and into heads.

Love Letters

I softly anchor you to feeling
that this too, dear one, shall pass
and pent-up sorrows from a lifetime
are given form and voice and space.

I will never forsake your call,
and long-suffering I will soothe.
We are never truly parted,
It's important to know the Truth.

Do not linger over-long.
Do not overstay your time.
I so ably give you your due
but then you need to give me mine.

And it is the warmth of my enfoldment
which holds your heart and soul so dear,
as your storm is given safe passage,
the next step becomes ever clear.

With each lingering breath of acceptance,
with each comfort in the climb,
my wings lift you when you falter,
my embrace shelters you over time.

Spent, you sleep deeply,
in the harbour of my care.
Stay awhile...just stay awhile
and I will cherish you while there.

Love,
All of Love

About Joy

Dear Bursting Souls,

When you remember to enjoy what fuels your passion, you are in joy. Being joyful is not the same as feeling happy. Being happy is that feeling that arises from having something positively satisfied, tending to involve more superficial activities like acquiring things or deriving pleasure from and with others.

Experiencing joy comes from deep within. It is that profound feeling that is maintained no matter what external circumstances transpire. It is that motivator when we are imprisoned in our minds, bodies, or spirits. It is that deep connection to the source of all Love and acceptance.

When people demonstrate such luminescent elation, they are sharing flashes of their souls...for the soul is liberated, no matter how contained is the mind and body.

Joy-full people shine with luminosity. They always seek to radiate that which glows from within. Some may externalize their merriment, with a Tiggerific bounce and exuberance that is at once infectious, playful, and warm. Their sunshine smiles dispel gloomy thoughts and lift spirits.

Others may share a jubilance that is subtle, silently radiating outwards, drawing others towards them. They magnetize those who seek to drink in their understated energy and all feel uplifted and warm as a result.

People, though, cannot readily explain the precise quality of the more introverted, effervescent soul, as it resides more in the sublime. But their smiles and fond recognition are proof enough that joy has touched lives around those who celebrate its resting-place within them.

How can we create more bliss in our lives?

When we accept that we are deeply loved, just as we are, with no hoops through which to jump…we are enraptured by joy. When we can accept and value others for who they are, just as they are, experiencing the freedom of that choice…joy floods in. When we look at the natural world around us, with eyes unblemished by cynicism, seeing all things with the wonder and delight of a child...we erupt with joy.

If you were to take a pebble from the ground and imagine all of the centuries of hard conditions that whittled down that pebble from its original boulder, you would know how relentlessly taxing circumstances can carve you to the core of who you are. Recognize that you also have a larger context in your natural surroundings.

Each of us belongs. Each of us has something unique to contribute. We matter because we are matter. And it matters that we matter. How joyous a thought indeed!

Joy, then, arrives in each moment that we choose to remember we are all connected and necessary threads in the fabric of Life.

It is also exponentially multiplied when given away. Joy begets more joy, just as Love begets more Love. Who would then willingly refuse more joy or Love entering into their lives?

Yet, so often, we neglect to find ecstasy in our daily routines. We take for granted our physical abilities, our loved ones, our Selves.

Joy waits patiently, though, within a renewed heart, a discerning mind, a well-intentioned comment, a sincere hug, a prayerful litany of gratitude, and in the company of our angels. Joy, then, is always readily near.

May elation trickle or rush into your spirit today.

May you be filled to overflowing with the blessedness that Joy brings.

May the feeling of rapture permanently rupture the wall that separates you from everyone else and find a forever home within you.

Ecstatically yours,
Love

To Procrastination

Dear "I'll Do It Tomorrow" Follower,

So many times, a burst of energy and excitement sparks the beginning of a new project or idea...only to stumble back into relative obscurity or stacks of unwritten paper. What do you wish to convey while you create and accumulate *to do* lists?

There is so much Life to continue to share and here you are: daydreaming, playing on Facebook, or putting off something that would help clear out the old and make way for the new.

At what point does exercising patience and allowing events to unfold become delaying and resisting? Would you know what makes the difference?

It is important to pay attention to the clues, to go deeper into that space of delay, recognizing patterns and rooting out old beliefs that seem to underscore decisions and half-lived lives.

Where did that initial fervor go? What needs greater loving, in order to complete a longer-term project or something as seemingly simple as going through boxes, discarding all that no longer serves?

What does holding on *do*, exactly? As if by holding on, there is some unspoken attempt to stop time from marching on or change from inevitably happening?

So many questions seek resolution, without the benefit of a sense of satisfaction when a job is finally completed. If I could love you through your apathy, would that help clear your way?

Let me shore up your confidence, removing all doubt and feelings of unworthiness. Let my loving energy move through you, finding completion in a process of healing that…

And that was where I left off in the sentence, right in the middle of writing it!

Oh, there was a sudden phone call to answer; random calls to make to loved ones; dishes to wash; laundry to do; every conceivable task and non-task that also delayed the completion of this Love letter! Many hours later, I completed it….

Love Letters

It is apparent how easy the distractions can be. They are as simple as *Don't see me*. What would I *see* if I caught you long enough to pay attention to your lack of attention?

Would I see your sense of inadequacy? Or how about your fear? Would you be willing to show me where you hurt...after risking so much, so often? Are you overtired from things ending, when you just want good things to remain? Have there simply been too many disappointments and not enough WOO-HOOs?

Or does it only feel that way sometimes? I *love* what I see:

- ❤ the resident beauty of your exuberance,
- ❤ the thrill of emerging ideas,
- ❤ all your creative babies-in-the-making, and
- ❤ your child-like wonder.

Perseverance is there too, as you *do* achieve what you set out to do, weighing and balancing choices and saying "no" when it is necessary.

You soldier on, especially when it matters the most. Your heaviness is less weighty when you ask for help or you admit that some tasks are overwhelming. Instead, practice asking for what you need and accepting help. It is time you realize that you do not need to be perfect, nor does everything you do have to be done perfectly.

When you take one small step towards your goal, think of a treat you can give yourself! I am so grateful that I am getting to know you, so we can work together towards completion.

I am not leaving. I have never gone. And I will be with you always as you continue this journey of endings, beginnings, beginnings, and endings.

Love you forever, especially when you want to stall,
Love

On Taking Action

Dear Determined Ones,

There is nothing more exhilarating than when you put movement behind a decision. Acting on one small (or not so small) goal puts you in the driver's seat of your own life, where you can control whether or not things stay the same or change.

How cool is that?! What excitement bursts forth when you make that phone call, write that e-mail, or initiate that conversation.

When you leave the couch behind and follow through on something thought about, that feeling swells in your chest and creates its own burgeoning momentum.

A thrilling ride ensues. And in that only-the-Universe-knows way, that one action sets up a domino effect. Miracles happen. Doors open. Opportunities arise. People who can help begin to appear to propel you along.

Cheerleading happens when it is most necessary. A song plays that offers you encouragement. A seminar connected to your project comes into your possession and you continue along, buoyed—not giving up, giving in, or throwing in the towel. Not this time.

Sometimes, it is important to shore up your strength and take the time required to prepare for that step.

Other times, it is the immediacy of a circumstance that requires that you say "Yes!" and do something right then.

Still other times, it is practice, practice, practice, where you keep at the same discipline so that it becomes second nature and naturally improves.

And that repetition guarantees the promise of achieving excellence.

Word by word: that is the way to forge a book or a letter, poem, essay, article, monologue, or movie.

One word. Followed by another. Moved along by your hand writing or hands typing, as if taking dictation from a Divine Muse. Quel amuse!

And do not forget to have fun! See each part as an experiment in this Laboratory called Life.

Scientists do not avoid mistakes and neither should you. Experimenters test theories. Not having the expected outcome does not nullify an experiment but gives valuable information for the next approach, so they can determine what changes and what stays the same.

What say you? Are you willing to toss aside your preconceived notions of success or your fear of looking ridiculous or falling on your face in order to try something different?

The doing *is* the trying and that is why it does not fail. Predictable future results occur because of past successful performance.

Action! Galvanizing into action causes your soul to sing and your body to rise to the occasion.

What a happy day it is when what we think about doing gets done. *Now* is a moment of decisive action. There is no neutral in now. Moving from a thought to a realized outcome is cause for the biggest *Woo-Hoo!*

When you ask questions, offer new perspectives, brainstorm, network, and follow through with action, you are an agent of change. For each new idea or decision automatically introduces a shift in the way you think and behave. Change may be scary but you are designed to handle it. The greatest satisfaction follows the most intense commitment.

Saying "I do" is making your own vow. Wow!

Love to celebrate you at your own finish line,
Love

To (Imp)atience

Dear (Imp)atience,

Oh, you little imp! How many times have we had this conversation, the one where I remind you that it is a virtue to exercise Patience?

Where does this frustration with delay come from? If you were to source this feeling, perhaps you would find the answer for every time you grow agitated, afraid, and start to lose peace when what you were expecting to happen does not occur. But you can never catch a fish without first growing still.

This is a familiar feeling, isn't it? Being unable to control circumstances, another's behaviour, or their timetable…or God's work: one according to a Divine plan.

What is that concept of time for you? Are you at odds with your own natural ebb and flow? With how Life unfolds? With being told to wait? Or not knowing when something will happen, so you can be ready... especially if a disaster strikes?

This is a perfect opportunity to exercise acceptance. Release. Allow Grace to come into your space and linger awhile...a long while.

What would you do if you relaxed into this new-found free time? Think of all of that you could pursue or finish. Imagine what Life would be like without being held hostage to time? Or not having your nervous, uptight energy coursing through a poor, unsuspecting person because you are basically free from errant thoughts and feelings that are stuck in past events... never the present?

A fleeting feeling of edginess is understandable, but being frozen by this all-consuming flood of past living is really a prescription for dis-ease. At the very least, it is a nagging inconvenience that demonstrates an area requiring maturing. At most, it is a deadly cocktail of stress that is sure to shorten a life.

So, where *do* you come from? Is it an individual experience to ferret out, or are there common experiences that resonate with many?

Are you about a time that someone said they would do something and failed to do it? That disappointment brought up feelings of rejection, neglect, pain, a sense that someone did not feel cared for or about?

Or perhaps you were triggered when needs were not met and a feeling of doom cast its grey pall on things? Or how about the feeling of intense disappointment when trusting someone to do what they said they would do, only to find out that their actions did not match their words?

Does someone's peace of mind have to be tied to the arrival of an anticipated need?

(Imp)atience, is it possible that you are activated when someone puts all of their eggs in someone else's basket, depending overly much on what another says or does?

When you externalize your well-being and make events or others responsible, you put too much pressure on the process that needs to unfold organically. It is a set-up that will always fail, as you will always lose your serenity and equilibrium doing that.

You need to lighten up! Let go! Allow. Take better care of yourself and watch how much happier and more peaceful you become.

Thank you for these important reminders. (Imp)atience, you become *I'm patience* with the appropriate time and space! You just did not know it before now.

But now that you do...you can delight in the freedom that this knowledge brings!

Love you for the messages you bring,
Love

To Share Serenity

Dear Serene Souls,

When you settle into that space of complete calm, quietude envelops every worry, challenge, or over-active imagination. When there is no need to hurry or do, serenity has taken hold of you—and it is a capture that is not resisted, but welcomed.

It is as still as a dew-misted lake, where the air itself seems suspended, not wanting to disturb the reverence of the moment.

No news of distress or agitation can shake that inner sense of such Divine soothing that a peaceful heart beats ever-so-softly; each surrounded by the protection of a thousand angels, and all is viewed with kindness, detachment, and Love.

No judgments are levied, no defenses are mounted, only confidence in the natural unfolding of a life without the need to obsess, fear, and control.

What does this level of sereneness feel like? It is in the calming sigh of the wind after a whirlwind day, or the blessed contentment that arrives when a sleeping baby is held. It is in the sacred connection during silent prayer or meditation.

Serenity is in the interruption of hurtful thoughts before being uttered at another, or in the drowsy self-content upon waking after a restful, deep sleep. It is found in the comfort of stroking a beloved pet, or being awash in relaxation, when immersed in a creative hobby, passion, or the sun's healing light. Divine nurture occurs in Nature, where it stills a frenzied mind.

What creates a serene soul? Serenity can arrive after a heart-to-heart communication with a loved one, where acceptance and care are declared, as if telling untold secrets sets us free and puts emotions at rest.

Love-making and sharing can bring contentment, as spiritual and sexual energies find release in being completely naked and vulnerable in one of the deepest displays of intimacy.

Meditation, restorative retreats, prayer, Tai chi, Qigong, yoga, fellowship, creative spurts, a walk in

Love Letters

Nature, the symbolic action of plunging into water and slicing through the resistance, listening to a slow-tempo song, or singing a soothing lullabye—there are so many ways to foster serenity.

There are as many avenues of accessing this inner space of calm as there are individual preferences. Just know that when you enter that sacred sanctuary, nothing easily rivals its healing effects.

What if we regularly or frequently found ourselves blessed by basking in this unflappable and consistent energy? How would our lives unfold? What miracles would occur in changed hearts and healed hurts?

There is so much tranquility available. Let us meet in the heart space of eternity that serenity brings!

Love,
Love

On Rainy-Day Boredom

Dear Saturated Souls,

When ominous clouds roll in and the sun is blocked from view, all outdoor activities are kept on *stand-by* until the first drops of rain confirm the deluge that ends those events.

Some will curse the sky for its betrayal. Others will welcome the release. After all, lawns need watering and people need a break from a heat wave.

Then the tinnish tock, plunk, tock of raindrops sound against roofs and windows, a hypnotic pattern that lulls one to sleep. The grey casts its pall inside rooms that can no longer depend on natural light to illuminate indoors. Lights click on and hearts are invited to click open.

Love Letters

What to do on a rainy day? Perhaps time to catch up on reading, sleeping, or lying languidly in bed, making love with that special someone. Or huddle, snuggled under a comfy comforter and watch a favourite movie, or reach out to a distant friend by phone, or empty neglected boxes, drawers, or closets.

Do these days give us time to bake a pie or contemplate the echoes in our minds since we cannot remain preoccupied with the busy chores of an interrupted day? Do we feel guilty or grateful during rainy days—or a little bit of both?

Do we arm ourselves as we brave the onslaught of relentless raindrops, fool's folly to even remotely attempt to dodge them when we venture outdoors?

How important are groceries or the consumer lists to be filled, when puddles pool on the ground and in our memories of past sodden excursions?

What if we took this time out from distractions to connect to that which calls forth expression? Rainy days beckon us to tune in. Let us notice our breathing, which automatically expands and contracts our lungs. Let us be deeply grateful for this natural occurrence, which we take for granted on most days.

Let us remember days gone by, filled with rainy day memories...usually involving summertime family games. Or how about lolling around without a care in the world, contentment seeping in as easily as the rain?

Let us be thankful for this time to just *be*, finding the resident peace and Love that is always there for our refreshment and sustenance. Let us drink our fill of *down* time, not to bring us down, but to help us replenish our energy. Rainy days are golden days. All we have to do is be mindful of the gifts they bring. And be open to receiving what we are given, passing along our gifts to others...especially during their rainy days!

Love,
A Fellow Saturated Soul

To Create Curiosity

Dear Curious Souls,

Remember what it was like as a child the first time you thought of doing something new that you wanted to do?

It could have been learning to ride a bike, or joining a sports team, or reading by yourself, or savouring your first kiss.

There was an idea that you heard, read about, or saw, and you felt butterflies in your stomach. Your face visibly showed enthusiasmos (*God within*) and something resonated so deeply inside of you that it stirred you, taking up residence in your mind, body, and heart.

Some of you could think of nothing else, so consumed by the energy of your new-found passion: whether it was music, academics, visual arts, sports, movement, a complex design, languages, or a limitless array of interests.

A bursting-open-mind followed the faintest knowledge, with a thirst to know and learn more about your bliss.

Young children are inherently curious and grow easily animated when they are exploring something new.

An infant will stare for long moments at an object until eventually an uncoordinated hand, finger, foot, or mouth will attempt to capture that which has been so captivating.

Humans strive for ever new understanding, information, ways to improve, and master our environment—both internal and external.

Who remembers cracking open the spine of a long-coveted book that you eagerly, yet impatiently, waited to read? Oh, the smell of freshly printed paper and the words that jumped up and catapulted your imagination into another world. Yes!

Or, with a pencil in hand, the picture that appeared almost miraculously from a blank page?

Do you remember the courage it took to risk failing at something over and over again before you finally succeeded, practicing it into near-perfection? The exhilaration throughout your body matched the extra aliveness you felt, the sparkle you exuded, and the infectious energy you radiated.

What about the fearlessness it took (and takes) to embrace something painful, yet by doing so, you are able to discipline yourself toward a new habit or way of thinking and being? What would it feel like to have a beginner's attitude toward life again?

Of all the gazillion new things to experience and learn, it would hardly seem possible that you could feel bored. So there is nothing the matter with becoming childlike again. It is even more enjoyable since you can use your adult understanding to appreciate what a gift a seeker's attitude can have to remain young at heart.

Well then, off you go,
Love

To Deal With Doubt

Dear Doubtful Heart,

There are so many times that you forget I exist. By comparing yourself to others, you come up lacking, which sets off a round of rapid-fire ammunition against your capabilities, wonderful qualities, and the uniqueness of remarkable *you*.

Your willingness to be open sets you up for the questions that others pose to you, when they express their doubts about new ideas or projects.

Can you achieve what you state you want to do? How can you handle the "what ifs" that others throw at you, which suggest that they do not believe you have thought through all of the possible things that could go wrong with a particular goal or plan?

What if what you set out to achieve was successful, rather than a failure, or incomplete?

What if you could focus on building a solid foundation to pre-empt possible set-backs?

What if you gathered forces around you who supported your vision and offered to provide positive, exciting feedback, and creative problem-solving?

What if you believed in yourself enough to trust that you would seek the help you need, so you could build great learning opportunities?

Are you prepared to handle all of Life's achievements or only the setbacks and failures?

Where does uncertainty lead you?

Doubt...it is a familiar road you travel and you can stumble in the potholes, stuck along that weary way, downtrodden instead of vibrantly strong.

There was a time when you, Doubt, had little airplay, when confidence led the way and results supported healthy choices and creative passions.

How did you now get star billing? You are welcome in this family of emotions, however, it is always a blessing when your silence stands out.

For in quietness, other feelings and actions can dictate the fulfillment of a plan.

You strongly support those other feelings when you lend your will to them rather than calling so much attention to uncertainty. You love the mysterious unknown and there is an incredible amount of resident potential and excitement there!

It is as if you can provide a bird's eye view of what it is like to be in that go-between place, where both paths of a choice may be seen.

Put your shoulder into making others question their motives for being the voices of reason without enough deep inquiry. You can inspire them to doubt why they doubt!

For if these others pondered a circumstance more closely, they would realize that they are not the authority on the outcome…that decision is left to the one who came up with the idea. You are the creator of the outcome.

You have more power than you realize. You just need to take it back. Transformation usually occurs through the power of consistent decisions. Seek out others who can help you reinforce the links of confidence so that they remain unbroken.

Love Letters

And Doubt, do not give credence to those *nay-sayers* who seek to still...but do not allow them to break...your rattled chain.
You can do this!

Sending supportive comfort,
Love

To Embrace Hope

Dear Hope-Full Ones,

When we take a look around us, let us see our circumstances, loved ones, and possibilities as if they are improving in that moment. For they may well be.

Hope is the blanket in which we wrap ourselves at night, especially when the darkest time seems the longest.

It is the beacon which keeps our dreams in sight, while Love and passion are the fuel that propel us ever forward.

The optimist is always trusting that life is getting better, and a hopeful nature provides the foundation from which optimism can spring.

How is it that some can feel this energy of positivity while others cannot?

If you are one who easily feels discouraged or beaten down, it is understandable that you may need some extra help to recover a forward-looking attitude.

Think of developing an *all things are possible* perspective and then handle challenges as if you are looking for buried treasure. Imagine digging and digging, and it seems that there is only dirt and darkness—and a whole lotta hard work—and the hole grows deeper, that is when a useful *time out* can be called. Then it is time to take stock and discover what to do next. The map needs to be reviewed. Was there a mistake in reading the directions? Are you where you need to be?

Rather than getting upset that you have not discovered the treasure yet, focus on what is working. Taking an objective view of your situation, you can more easily spot what the delay is about and calmly set about adjusting, then breaking down the steps that are required to re-solve the issue.

Celebrating or recognizing that you have a decent shovel, great stamina, your provisions to keep you going, whoever may be willing to support you—all of the blessings for which you can be grateful—all of these things inspire hope.

By reminding yourself of these important aspects of your experience, you can garner confident faith that you will find your treasure.

Taking stock, then taking steps, gives you renewed energy and the determination to move forward with the feeling and belief that you WILL find your hidden treasure.

And how do you know that today will not be the day you find it?

If not, continue to move forward anyway. It is so important. And so is determining whether your expectations are true and reasonable or if you have misplaced your internal compass.

So many times, we think we know what is best for ourselves and our hope becomes geared towards something that cannot happen. And never will.

It is as if we believe there is a buried treasure because someone told us it was there, but we have no map and no way of determining if what they told us is a Truth or a lie.

Hope is an amazing and miraculous agent of change and one that keeps all other parts of our thinking and living operational.

Love Letters

Without optimism, especially during intense challenges, we would not be able to function. Our minds dictate how our bodies feel and we need to feel that no matter what, we are going to be okay. The Truth is that we can handle whatever happens. We are never alone and we do not have to pretend to be.

May Hope make its home inside each of us. Not to delude us with fairy-tale dreams and hints of buried treasure, but as the driver in the process of change: changed viewpoints, perspectives, judgments, feelings, willingness, opportunities, Love.

Trusting that you know how much you are loved,
Love

About Stress and Overwhelm

Dear Frazzled Souls,

Here it is again. That same wound-up feeling, like an overly-taut guitar string before it snaps.

Nerves all buzzing inside as thoughts go around in the mind like an endless merry-go-round: *Gotta get this chore done. Finish that project. Don't forget to pick up the groceries. Get dinner made. Damn the rush hour traffic! It's a rat-race out there. Stop feeling dizzy. You can't get things done right. When was the last time you did everything you said you were going to do? Pick up the pace.*

The tears may not poke through the surface. But what about that gnawing pain in your neck? Or the headache ready to explode into a full-blown migraine? How about that knot in your gut, or the sore muscles from clenching and holding up what feels like the weight of the world, at least your world of responsibilities? One wrong move and the whole house of cards will collapse.

What if they tell you they do not love you? Or they do not want you to hang around anymore? Your family, who does not understand you, so they shun you. Or that circle of friends whose lives are neat, orderly, and predictable, unlike yours. And work demands that pile up in front of you.

Membership has its privileges. Yet you do not feel that people are pulling their load. But they know you will, so they expect you to do it and make everything okay.

But are you okay? When did you consciously sign up for doing everything? Isn't parenthood shared? Single parenthood is like doing double duty, usually with less than half of the resources.

No complaints about the choices that were made, just the lived experience of stress on top of stress.

Researchers say that you need some stress to actually live a vibrant life.

But when does stress become overwhelm? When finances are tight. Or non-existent. Or there is no room-to-breathe-because-deadlines-are-looming-and-nights-are-sleepless-and-mostly-everyone-else-you-meet-has-that-edge-to-their-voice-and-you-think-that-everyone-is-getting-on-everyone-else's-last-nerve-too.

Life is not fair when you are this strained and overwhelmed. Life is not what you thought it would be. You thought the world would offer more kindness and acceptance. More offers to help. More resources. More. Not less. Or nothing.

Then again, when was the last time you offered to pick up someone else's mess? Or volunteer?

Or perhaps you piled more on top of more and you are more upset with yourself that you could not say "no." Or "not yet."

But why do most say "no" to you? Is it because you have looked and acted so strong for so long that they do not think you need the help? Or is it because they are afraid you are too needy and would be a never-ending drain?

Did you ask them or have you expected them to read your mind? But can't they tell you are out of sorts, preoccupied, and too self-focused?

Love Letters

So what do you do, when you feel torn into a million pieces? Try slowing everything down. Stay focused, right here, right now. What is your body feeling? What is it trying to tell you? Where is the tension?

Can you take a deep, deep breath, hold it and exhale slowly? How about getting a cup of herbal tea? No caffeine, no nicotine, no sugar, or energy drinks, nothing that artificially increases your heart rate, even though you think it gives you energy. The crash always arrives and makes things worse. That only adds to your exhaustion.

When was the last time you told yourself "I love you?" Or you told someone else and then asked for a hug?

Rather than repeating a litany of undone duties, what would being loving toward yourself accomplish? Could that bring tears to the surface? Perhaps they need to be shed. Toxins are released through tears. Better they are expelled from you than kept inside your body.

Do you know the last time you appreciated all of your hard work, unfinished though it may be? Removing the expectation that others would notice and thank you also removes resentment and extra stress.

You do a good job. You do a lot. You are doing the best you can right now. So for the next ten minutes, how about you just sit quietly and give yourself a pat on the back? If ten minutes is too long, start with one minute of appreciative thoughts that celebrate *you*.

What would cheer-leading for yourself sound like? Look like? *Feel like?*

Is it a walk in a favourite place, like a park, or listening to your favourite music, or digging in your garden? Is it buying yourself some flowers, taking a bath, getting a massage, manicure, or pedicure? Is it skipping a rope or skimming a stone across a lake or pumping weights? Is it going for a swim, getting your haircut, visiting with a friend you have not seen in awhile? Is it a trip to a museum, library, art gallery, flea market, or craft store? Or going to a field and throwing or kicking a ball around? Is it a counselling appointment where you learn new coping strategies? Is it holding a hand or sharing a hug?

For each and every one of us, there is something healthy that reduces stress, that helps put our overload into perspective.

No matter what you do, decide you are worth it. Because you are. Because there isn't another person like you in the whole world. And there would be a hole if you were no longer here.

And taking care of yourself is the best gift you can give to yourself and your loved ones, even when you say "no." Saying "no" means that they will need to learn to do some things. You slowing down helps them grow up.

And everyone needs to do their part to contribute. Feeling overwhelmed is like the light indicator displaying on the dashboard of a vehicle. It is the warning to get a system check before your engine breaks down. Or worse…you.

Trusting that you will *take* care, and not wait for it to be handed to you,
Love

On Surrender

Dear Souls Who Seek the Sanctuary of Surrender and Silence,

Surrendering to that which we cannot control is such a sweet and powerful release. Letting go of those extra activities or over-commitments helps bring us back to a place of balance. In our world of technological advancement, we are hard-pressed to sit in a complete absence of noise. Usually, faint humming and buzzing can be heard and they have a discordant and distracting effect—much like the droning of a fly or a bee. To be fair to bees and flies, they usually fly away and their sounds fly with them.

When we find ourselves in a place of respite—commonly in natural surroundings—we experience what is termed the *profound of silence*. There is something blessed about the sounds of Nature, with each creature communicating in its own unique way.

Time feels suspended while a uniform quiet descends. Even the leaves cease their busy waving. The sun cuts a swath of light through the trees and its heat penetrates to the core. Brain wave activity measurably slows down—a trance-like state ensues. Thoughts meander in and out—but mostly out.

In this no-place of stillness, molecules merge, as all is embraced in Oneness. In that merging is a keen sense of connection with forces seen and unseen, frequencies heard and not heard, moments measured and unmeasured. A deep resonance with and reverence for all of Life is felt, not just through the body, but throughout the mind and spirit. It is as if, in this silence, there are no separations between the finite world and the place of infinity. Eternity lives in each of us. Eternity resides around us. Eternity *is* us.

In this hush, there is no delineation of where *you* begin and end. The distinction as a separate being is a construct designed to place us in our flesh-and-blood experience. On a deeper level, however, we are always joined together—with everything—a blissful union so complete that we instinctively know that we belong, we are safe, welcome, and home.

May all of us experience this profound affinity with everything around us. May we remain mindful of its existence, aware that what we do to one another, we do to ourselves and our world, so we can discipline ourselves to commit to *do no harm*. Then can we celebrate the feeling that the miraculous resounds in the solace of silence and in the relief of giving up that which does not serve.

In quietude,
Love

To Pain

Dear Visitor,

You arrive suddenly in the body and make an announcement that you are there: either acutely flaring up, slicing into consciousness, or as a chronic, achy feeling.

Your arrival is not usually welcome, as there are chores to do, people to see, plans that need adjusting or canceling, depending on your severity.

However unwelcome you may be, there is always new information learned when you are asked: "What do you want to communicate? What do you need?"

Sometimes, medication is the antidote that solves your crisis and the body returns to health. Other times, it is through deep breathing, visualization, a soothing bath, massage, reiki, reflexology, Emotional Freedom Technique (tapping), Emotion Code practice, Real Love retreats, going to Heal spa, acupuncture, prayers, chiropractic, meditation and music, and other healing modalities. By paying attention to the body's cues and responding in a way that seeks to release stored energy, Pain, you are no longer trapped and can be released.

There is much we do not yet understand concerning the subtlety of your arrival and the influence that thoughts and feelings have on the body.

Some of the many causes and conditions which create disharmony and disrupt the natural flow within the body include:

- resentment, fear, anger, disappointment, envy, jealousy, shyness, stress, sadness,
- excitability, chronic loneliness, nervousness, depression, abuse, doomsday dread,
- pessimism, unworthiness, shame, blame, judgment, criticism, denial, repression,
- superiority, arrogance, lust, greed, procrastination, aversion, tension, futility, resignation, guilt,
- competition, unwillingness, control, aggression, addictions, negativity, unforgiveness,

- ❤ lack, over-indulgence, indecisiveness, stubbornness, obstinacy, degeneration, uncaring, trapped emotions,
- ❤ hostility, martyrdom, and victimization.

Pain, you provide a valuable service. You declare that *something* is wrong. You can be an agent of change, especially if there is a critical health issue that will not be sustained by the same lifestyle and patterns of thinking and action that caused it.

Relationships may need to be examined, especially the relationship with Self and the nastiness that can underpin unconscious thoughts.

Support and Love are always key contributors in addressing and healing pain. Embracing rather than resisting can also create relief and an improved outcome.

You are seen in your most vulnerable state, as you seek expression. You need to be paid attention to, validated, held and loved, even though you are not usually appreciated.

You have much to offer and, without you, the body may die before it is time, as you are the messenger that something is amiss. I gratefully acknowledge your contribution to well-being and greater care.

And what about the times when there is no pathological source of you, Pain, in the body, yet a person feels you? That is when you call for extra Love and kindness. For then you are reacting to thoughts and feelings that cause too much stress and heaviness of spirit. That is when you are amplified.

Let me cradle you in the warmth of my embrace. Let me soothe the woe that is so prevalent in you. Let me assure you that no matter what you reveal…you are cherished!

> It is a faith-full heart which knows no doubt.
> It is a hope-full heart which knows no limitation.
> It is a Love-filled heart which knows no fear.
> It is a forgiving and forgiven heart which knows
>   no pain.
> Let us experience the fullness of Faith, Hope,
>   Love, and Forgiveness!

Thank you, Pain, for your gift of communication and awareness. You can save lives, even though at times you overstay your welcome.

Love Letters

Practicing Gratitude and Forgiveness are the main antidotes to Pain. It is up to us to rewrite our stories and help is available so that we do not have to do it alone.

Wishing you blessings as you speedily depart.

Love,
Love

On For-Giveness

Dear Unreleased Souls,

Have you ever experienced the feeling of being flooded with resentment and dread and holding on tightly to past grievances like they were some sort of war wounds, all to identify how much you have been hurt?

Do you know what it feels like to be bloated with the past, unable to fully embrace and enjoy the present and the gifts that it brings?

What would it feel like to release those toxic memories and issues that clog up your body, mind, and spirit and instead feel the exquisite lightness of being that giving up this sludge would bring?

The word *forgiveness* has been misused and pre-empts a complete healing process. It has been tossed around to justify unacceptable behaviour without a clear path of understanding and compassion for what its process actually achieves.

People use forgiveness easily but still do not generate and find the release that they seek.

Let us look at for-giveness. When you do something as a way of giving, you give up that which holds *you* hostage, not the one who has been the agent of pain. We forget that when we have had an injustice levied on us we do not have to continue holding on to it. When we give up that which has been given to us, we are no longer bound to the certitude that pain has in our lives.

For-giveness, then, is a profound gift—used to release ourselves. It replaces the tight hold of an unresolved past by clearing it from within us. A forgiven heart is a healed heart. Forgiveness heals.

It is the greatest treasure we can experience and give to ourselves and the one that has the most profound, lasting effect.

When we are ready, we release what we have held on to for so long and that can be a scary proposition and exercise.

Let us look upon our world as if we truly belong in it and with each other. Let us find the blessings and Love that we share, rather than focusing on the superficial ideologies that we do not. Dogmas do not heal hearts! But understanding, compassion, forgiveness, wisdom, cooperation, collaboration, tolerance, peaceful co-existence, and our willingness to create positive change can all contribute to a healed world!

Forgiveness is a two-part process:

1. Release that which holds you hostage to a hurt.
2. Remember to Love.

Let us resolve to re-solve those areas that have created pain, challenge, and a lack of forgiveness within us.

Let us resolve to live our lives as if what we thought, said, and did matter...they do.

Let us embrace all of the yumminess of life and share the yummiest Love...for that can feel so good.

Give the gifts that keep on giving: Grace, Forgiveness, Gratitude, and Love! Each new day offers us a clean slate upon which we can write something fresh...and miraculously different from any previous day.

Meeting another in our heart-space is the closest we come to each other and God.

God is always in our heart-space and the door is always open. Each circumstance in life, no matter how painful or repetitive, bears the gifts of understanding and compassion.

Gratitude keeps us hopeful.
Hope keeps us grateful.
Forgiveness keeps us humble.
Humility helps us forgive.

Forgiveness could actually be termed for-give-more! When we give, we can give-more!

When we practice self-forgiveness, we can forgive any transgression against us.

Just as your hand clenches around a coin, when you release your grip and the coin falls, there is an unnatural feeling, as the blood flows back to your hand...so too with for-giveness.

What do you replace your resentments with... especially when they have taken up so much of your space, time, and energy?

There may be emptiness. It may be easier to want to retrieve the same thoughts, feelings, memories, and behaviours to which you have grown accustomed. The discipline of expressing gratitude and Love will contribute enormously in helping replace the space left open by forgiveness.

Imagine if you gave every cell in your body Love and appreciation when you feel inclined to start replaying past injustices.

Imagine the freedom that would enter your body, mind, and spirit. Instead of heading down a path of destructive thoughts (stinkin' thinkin'), you choose a path of life filled with constructive thoughts.

What kind of world would we have if we for-gave? If we for-give?

A life brimming with beauty, harmony, peace, contentment, Love, and endless possibility is much more exciting and energizing than life engorged with pain, bitterness, and the litany of *look what they did to me*. Or more painful yet, *look what I did to myself...again*.

We can hardly achieve much of anything if we are held hostage by what we have done incorrectly or what others have done in error.

Let us honour who we are and why we are here: to learn, grow, and share what we know. Every circumstance offers us a miracle: a changed viewpoint, a clear direction we choose to move into, the fortitude and strength of not playing a victim, the beneficent feelings of mercy, Trust, acceptance, and Love!

Let us transcend that which seeks to keep us small, wounded, and locked into victim thinking so that we may embrace our grand natures, our total God-selves.

Let us know that we come from a place of rightness and expansion, so we can shine the most brightly. Let us see and feel our lightness.

Let us always be mindful how subtle the tendency is to keep track of misdeeds. Let us embrace the lessons we learn from animosity and memory so that we can let them go.

Allow all of these masterful feelings to fill every one of us, returning us to a state of grace, acceptance, and energized commitment to release and move on. Each time we are faced with an *ouchie* in life, caused by ourselves, another, or both, know that we are for-given and we are called to for-give.

For-giveness is the key that sets us free and Love is the current that carries us.

Love in letting go,
Love

To Process Shame and Blame

Dear Shackled Souls,

Shame and blame can be called the destructive duo. They gnaw at our confidence, eat at our inner compass, erode our peace of mind, and become so entrenched in our subconscious that rooting them out requires delicate handling, like an archeologist who brushes away thousands of years of soil from a single bone fragment.

Much as digging at a dandelion's gnarly roots involves deft maneuvering or they will grow back, so do shame and blame's branched tendrils attach into the very heart of who we are.

Seeds are buried when we are young, usually during intensely traumatic experiences. We are unable to recognize someone else's lack of responsibility and so take it on as our own fault.

Another's shame and blame plants deep within us. Their words, directed at us, become the unconscious mantras that operate in our lives. We hear messages like: "You are worthless. You don't belong here. There's something wrong with you. Keep our little secret between us. Who do you think you are? You can't do anything right. What makes you think you can do that? You make me sick. Talk to someone who cares. You're always getting in trouble. Grow up. Leave me alone," and a thousand and one other variations of "I cannot love you as you are."

Adult actions, usually by someone in a position of authority, subject us to treatment that defiles our sense of vulnerability, trust, and innocence. Their abuse is branded into our skin. Our cells remember what we may not be able to consciously believe about ourselves.

Our tears, terrors, rage, bitterness, sense of injustice, and outrage are stuffed down even when we try to assert who we know we are.

The trusting optimist believes that most people—parents, teachers, older siblings, babysitters, clergy, doctors—or anyone in a position of authority over children, are well-intended when they want us to behave.

Those who flaunt this authority and abuse this trust are detrimental to others if they do not realize that attaching a child's behaviour to who they are does not create healthy, loving, balanced, or productive adults.

When the focus is mainly on what someone does wrong and, because of that, who they are is wrong, or fundamentally flawed, then shame and blame take root and flourish.

Shame's message: *Who we are is not okay.*

That belief then manifests into,

Blame's message: *What we do is not okay.*

Children do not have the internal mechanism to understand that shame and blame are seriously flawed ways of teaching proper conduct or instilling values.

These then become default settings, always ready to look at who is at fault—the individual or others—or both.

And these are never correct as a means of correction.

If the Truth is necessary to see a behaviour that requires adjusting, when shame and blame arrive, they hijack a person's ability to look at that behaviour, thus actually preventing change. These feelings are so intense that change is not possible with this destructive duo, much like a manicured lawn is not possible in the wake of a bumper crop of dandelions.

Rather than being motivators for healthy change, shame and blame shackle us. We feel small, stuck, afraid, and unable to take even one small step towards positive self-improvement.

Why?

There is no Love to be found in shaming and blaming. There is no room for error, growing, making mistakes, or being imperfect. There is no place to be human, to be our Selves.

Love removes shame and blame through objective Truth-seeking and telling. The Truth can be found in self-reflection, counselling, retreats, journaling, meditating, Real Love™ work, prayer, coaching, therapists, ministers, books, songs, and being with Love-filled people.

When we look at our behaviours as ways of being in the world, without attacking who we truly are (loved beyond imagination), we can determine if they are healthy or unhealthy. Put another way, we can ask ourselves the question: "Does this behaviour bring me closer to or further away from who I know my Self to be and how I want to share that with the world?"

We can then create manageable steps for change, ones that build in adjustments or room for errors, and also celebrate when we complete what we set out to do.

Positive affirmations and reinforcement counter-act feelings of worthlessness and shame. Taking responsibility for how we behave does not involve a *victim* or *abuser* mind-set.

If our choices create outcomes that are unhealthy, then we do not need to blame and shame ourselves or anyone else. We need to recognize what happened, identify what did not work, be accountable, and apologize (to ourselves and others, as long as doing so does not harm them). We must determine what needs to happen to prevent the same outcome from happening again, and then take an appropriate action to correct that.

This blueprint is not an intellectual or *touchy-feely* exercise. It requires doing something differently.

Love helps us see ourselves as whole individuals. Love illuminates those dark places within us and in our experiences. Not because we like to wallow in the dark, rather, so we can transform what was hidden into something new.

Love gives us the motivation and optimism to believe that change is not only possible, but do-able.

It reminds us that we are so much more than the sum-total of our character defects or challenges.

Love puts us in touch with our Divine natures, where acceptance is the first step towards healing. It roots out the untruths with the optimistic drive of a gardener in the spring.

And the destructive duo of shame and blame? Most importantly, Love transforms them into acceptance and taking responsibility.

Love Letters

May each of us know that we are wondrously made, perfectly imperfect, miracles of life. Let us proceed from these places and know that we each have something important to share with our Selves, each other, and our world.

Loving you to beyond,
Love

On Acceptance and Responsibility

Dear Ones Who Seek to Grow,

When we were very young and wanted to walk, we ventured to sit up without any support and, once we mastered that, we gained more strength in our arms and legs.

Through trial and error, we stood unsteadily and may have fallen (OUCH!!). But usually soothed, we would attempt walking again.

Then one day...we mastered it. Staying upright, albeit wobbly, we grasped the mechanics of balance and we learned a new skill.

Did we need to beat ourselves up because we fell down? Did adults think it was appropriate to berate a toddler because he or she was learning to walk? What expectation would there be that a young one would automatically, and in one day, be able to master such a technical skill as walking?

If anything, there were lots of loving words of encouragement, perhaps kisses on boo-boos, enthusiastic *oohs* and *ahhs* and laughter, as each attempt was observed.

As children, we experienced a rite of passage—several, actually—as we discovered new skills and explored the world around us. Acceptance, support, encouragement, and dogged perseverance followed us through the words and actions of those we sought to emulate: our parents, siblings, teachers, loved ones, and peers.

And so we grew. So, what has changed in our adult world, if we are learning new ways of thinking, feeling, and behaving? Do we not require acceptance and Love as we open a new chapter in our lives?

While it is important to have loved ones around us who love us no matter what, it is also vitally important we offer ourselves self-acceptance, especially during those fledgling steps towards change.

When we can embrace our weaknesses as naturally as we embrace our strengths, we are our most connected and authentic selves.

We can revel in our new-found and improved thoughts and behaviours, especially if they bring us to better and healthier outcomes in our relationships and lives.

Would it not be miraculous indeed, to celebrate each tentative step, as we metaphorically learn to walk, and with confidence, begin to run?

So what is the other part of the equation to healing and growing?

If acceptance is the first part, it is helpful to take responsibility for any mishaps or miss-takes along the way.

We demonstrate our maturity when we admit to ourselves and others when we have erred and are working on making positive changes in our lives.

Rather than making someone else responsible for how we think, feel, and act, we are much more empowered when we own what is ours to fix and change.

It is so refreshing, and such a relief, to clear up misunderstandings and seek ways to make amends if we have hurt another.

Love Letters

We live in the light of the Truth and Freedom when we acknowledge what we would like to change in ourselves and then go about doing that, through the transformative power of acceptance and the will to succeed in something that we were oblivious to before.

The statement *knowledge is power* is only part of the recipe for positive development. A climate that is conducive to experimenting and actions that create change all influence great achievement, as long as we have healthy self-assessment, loving feedback, and we can adjust our course through the very edifying route of taking responsibility.

The confidence we gain in doing this is of such value and is so powerful that we strengthen that muscle and become spiritual athletes in this game called Life.

So why don't we become as open, trusting, and inquisitive as a child learning to grow? Why don't we use the masterful tool of acceptance to promote advancement for ourselves and others?

Can we take responsibility when we have that steep learning curve and need to get back to the basics again?

Underneath all that we are discovering, practising, and implementing, can we show Love to others and ourselves? Not just when we are getting things right, but also when we are failing miserably?

Let us bring on a revolution of such internal proportion that it would finally, finally, shatter those out-dated and unhealthy tools of living and relating.

Is it not time to grow up by growing anew? Do we not deserve a different approach?

Let us try some new experiments in this Life laboratory. And let us be brave enough to continue pushing past resistance and failure until we succeed.

Love the new and improved you,
Love

From Guilt

Dear Tortured Souls,

When you make a mis-take, it is your healthy conscience that triggers my presence and prompts remedial action. I have a necessary but short-lived purpose.

However, if you have been raised to believe that who you are is woefully inadequate or intrinsically wrong, then I dredge up such a slimy sludge of dread over the slightest mishap that any possibility of repair quickly sinks into futility and despair.

I can overwhelm the senses with a flood of unrelenting judgments over past thoughts, actions, and errors. Questions and thoughts bombard: *"What if you had not...? How come you did not...? What were you thinking? Is it too late to...? Why did this happen? You never do anything right."*

Extraordinary Loving for Everyday Living

Each step of unmitigated suffering lands a soul closer to eternal exile. There is no escaping me when I am at my most extreme. I am a greedy and nasty master who takes every prisoner to task.

I am tenaciously attached to self-righteous and *holier-than-thou* attitudes, long-suffering martyrs who need a scapegoat, those who seek vengeance and unattainable perfection, and whose grief from tragedy is inconsolable.

Rarely am I kept in perspective, for it is far easier to make a mountain out of a mole hill than it is to look at a flaw with a clear perspective and work on fixing it. Seeing something from a rational view with the purpose of making amends does not have much (or any) chance when I am around. There is also no room for human error or repentance in the world of my making.

When you are all-consumed by my presence, if someone does something wrong you will feel sorry, even if you are not responsible for it. Feeling *less-than* is a constant state from which there is no release and I am a burdensome companion, unless drastic measures are taken to recognize and root me out.

Love Letters

There are some actions that have no redeemable purpose and I am brought to bear by those seeking redress. Someone must pay when something happens or goes horribly wrong. Too often, those who are at fault try to abdicate their rightful place when justice is served.

However, there is no real winner in a battle that uses me as its first line of defense. There is also no turning back along the path of recovery, as healing is the preferred outcome to any tragic event that gains too much of my focus.

May I only be administered in small doses, as I am a potent and deadly force that needs to be handled with great care.

Those with little Love available take great pains in whipping others into submission, while attempting to prove them unlovable. When someone uses me as a weapon, it is they who are most in need of kind reproach…and understanding…and compassion… and Love.

Let Love command its voice in the midst of their loudest condemnations, for it separates the deed from the doer and will always believe in the impossible, the miraculous, and the unknowable nature of forgiveness, grace, and Divine intervention.

During Life's journey, use me only for short periods, not as a long-suffering guide.

Love,
Guilt

About Innocence and Redemption

Dear Perfectly Imperfect Beings,

Living is not for the faint of heart. Every choice you make creates an outcome, either positive or negative. Every inaction or action sets in motion a series of events which affirms your Divine Self or confirms your most human self.

You cannot escape the Truth that you will make mis-takes as you live your life. Knowing that you can never be perfect, how do you navigate Life's storms and blessings?

Spiritual teachers and God-bearers throughout history have given us ways of living that seek to minimize pain and maximize Love, if you choose to seek out their messages.

When you see a newborn, it is easy to recognize how innocent, pure, and vulnerable he or she is. Each of you had that time when you were like a clean slate and the future was bright with promise. Do you remember a time when you were valued, appreciated, or especially loved? Having a rush of feel-good energy boosts confidence, lifts morale, and gives you strength to bear the difficult challenges that come along.

And yet, it is by going through the worst experiences that you are able to learn many of the *ouchies* to now avoid, as well as acquiring spiritual practices like letting go, for-giveness, empathy, compassion, kindness, grace, acceptance, and Love.

Unfortunately, the term is not called *growing joy* or *growing ease*, but it is called *growing pains*, for each pain holds within it the seed for deep change, greater awareness, and wisdom. However, continuing to recite a litany of past transgressions does not serve your growth, but stunts it. There is a huge difference between discernment and a healthy conscience and being wracked with guilt and having no remorse.

Love Letters

Living at peace with yourself involves riding the wave of human foibles, feeling the horror of your misdeeds and forgetting the past, but not the lessons.

If you do not have a healthy process for healing both what you do and what has been done to you, you guarantee a life of imprisonment. There are ways of making amends, being rehabilitated, and experiencing redemption.

There are those who try to instill guilt in another, but that is about their unwillingness to accept their own imperfection, so they shift responsibility onto one less able to stand up for him or herself.

At the deepest level, they believe the erroneous idea that they are above the law or so flawed that they can never change, so the risk of being vulnerable is futile. Their hearts have been walled off. They have not known what it is like to be unconditionally loved during their tender, formative years. They have been judged and labelled *bad* and unlovable and have lived out that message. So much hurt has been inflicted on others, causing suffering that can affect generation after generation. This sets in motion more pain, revenge, and a cycle of dysfunction that needs to finally be broken.

Love gives you the energy to free yourself from guilt. It helps you to reach out for healthy support, resources, and tools so that you can be responsible for your errors and bring grace into the depths of your suffering and the suffering of those around you. Love inspires you to tell the Truth so that the steps towards reconciliation can be put in motion.

There is no greater freedom than the one that has been hard-earned. Through all of the challenges, learning to have compassion and empathy for yourself gives you the capacity to be compassionate and empathetic towards others.

No human being is perfect. No human being will ever be perfect, which means that no one can really judge another. If you cannot walk a mile in another's shoes, then do not be so arrogant as to tell them what they should or should not be doing. You prevent them from learning how to walk and interrupt their soul development. Be willing to demonstrate humility, understanding, cooperation, kindness, empathy, compassion, and redemption.

Know that you come from a Divine Love that far surpasses our limited language to describe it. When you ask for healing and forgiveness, with a contrite heart, you will be heard. And you are never alone. Believe in miracles and do the work of atonement.

May your struggles be few and your loads be light. May you feel the healing presence of Divine Love in all that you do. May your choices bring you closer to Love, so that you are able to share that with everyone else. Know that you *can* be a force for positive change.

Loving you past your imperfection,
Love

To Fear

Dear False-Expectations-Appearing-Real,

It has been awhile since you last visited, but it is always noticeable when you are in human form: the staccato breathing, the darting of eyes, hands clenching and unclenching, little tremors twitching throughout a body, acid pooling in the stomach, and beading perspiration on cold palms.

There is also the *what-if* thinking, which always creates a catastrophic ending rather than an I-can-handle-it attitude.

Fear. You have much to teach us about what needs healing, what needs attention, and what resources are depleted when you turn your sudden appearance into a longer stay.

Once, you were absolutely essential when our ancestors' lives, their very survival, depended on quick wits, the response coming from their bodies with an adrenaline surge that kicked off the necessary fight-or-flight reaction.

However, this monumental wall of prolonged fight-or-flight that gets constructed and which prevents others from getting too close, does not serve a Life of Love.

In your grip, there is no relaxation, no rest, no chance to be truly authentic. You make it impossible to think clearly, as you flood the brain with chemicals and false messages that it is not safe to trust.

Yet you do an important job in ensuring that people are safe, but when you are in over-drive, constantly running the show, you drive everyone else away.

Do not feel threatened by Love. Do not avoid that which offers such nurturing and freedom. Being afraid to the point of distraction does not create healthy change.

Love seeks not to harm, but it does put you on notice.

Notice the beauty in the moments that are not life-threatening. Pay attention to the sights and sounds that emanate from one who loves. Observe the calm, the serene, the function of peace.

Breathe deeply in the knowledge that you are loved. Yes, you are loved and thanked for the message your arrival conveys.

Seek not to make a harbour in the heart, for you generate a long-suffering life when you brood.

Fear, you are not my enemy, for when I clasp you to me in the warmth and safety of my embrace, you settle down and accept.

And acceptance, dear Fear, is where all manner of change begins to happen. It is a marvel how by accepting you, I can deliver my greatest healing. Thank you, for shaking up the status quo!

Love to release you from yourself,
Love

On Love

Dear Lovers,

How can Love, such a monosyllabic word, denote such infinite forms of expression of a heart and a lifetime?

Love is warm and safe, like a soft puppy or kitten whose furry form is sheltered in the folds of a harbouring body. Love is vulnerable and nurturing—sometimes simultaneously.

Love is as majestic as a mountain, whose climbers seek fulfillment at the height of its challenge. It is also present in every emotion, thought, word, and deed, for its natural reflection is one of infinite giving, with fathomless and mystical depths into which we are summoned to plunge.

Love is as vast as the night sky, with millions of stars suspended, strings of lights that celebrate the universe in festive fashion. Love holds both light and dark, elements of contrast that identify wholeness and inclusion.

Its creative passion burns in the loins when lovers seek to fulfill each other's desires, for it is always in giving that one receives.

This benevolent and intense expression is easily transferred to writing a poem, drawing a picture, making windows of stained glass, vessels from clay, songs of spontaneous sounds, or dance out of subtle movements. The orgasmic relief is not only about sex, but about satisfying the creative craving and gifting its outcome to another or to the world.

Love croons lullabies to young and old, whether fussy or content, for the lyrical heart beats in unison through sound. Connection to another is bridged through music, imbued with the feeling that the other matters...deeply matters. Seeking to soothe, the spirit is solidly supported.

Love inspires feats of bravery, yearning to share through action what cannot be conveyed in thought alone. This feeling consumes then overflows in myriad forms of concrete expression.

Love Letters

Love is a thought, a feeling, a doing that seeks not its own gain but to give for the joy of giving.

Emptying then filling, the cycle of Love never ends. The Universe demonstrates that Love sustains us, through Nature, the creative force, the inspiration within our hearts, and deeds of such mastery that a single human would be incapable of completing them alone.

Through and with Love, we are both creator and created, embracing the contradiction of Life and savouring such sweet fullness that we cannot help but share what we make, have, and know with those around us.

For Love is an authentic Truth-telling, of and for each of us. That Truth: We come from the Creator's Love. We are loved. We share Love. And Love has no end.

Forever Loving You,
Love

Afterword: Resources

Dear Blessed Reader,

These are tumultuous and exciting times in which we are living. There are so many resources available for you to heal and pursue your passions and dreams. You are supported as never before, if you take the risk to ask. If you do not ask, you cannot receive.

As promised at the beginning of this book, I am including the contact information for the following people. They are miracle workers. They take your ideas and help make them a reality. And they do it with professionalism, hard work, creative wonder, passion, and Love. They believe in you, even when you may doubt your own capabilities. I am so thankful and grateful to have had their expertise in the birthing of this creative baby!

Love Letters

I am happy to present to you:

Dr. Judith Briles, founder of AuthorU and a New York Times best-selling author, helps writers become authors. She organized the AuthorU Extravaganza in Denver, Colorado, which I attended in May 2013 and is known as The Book Shepherd for a reason. She can be reached at: TheBookShepherd.com.

Nick Zelinger has so artfully, soulfully, and completely captured my intent with the book cover design. As an award-winning book cover designer, his work is masterful, creative, and I highly recommend him! I have felt so blessed by his talent and look forward to his eye-catching covers on the next book in this series. Please contact him through his website at: NZgraphics.com.

Ronnie Moore is a top-notch interior book design and book layout professional. She has been able to capture the essence of the material and match the font, spacing, and layout with such intuitive acumen that I am left in awe of her skill. She goes above and beyond in her quest for the exact look and style and is the perfect co-creator and mid-wife to help your creative baby emerge into the publishing world! You can contact her through her website: WESTypeBookDesigns.com.

My first contact editor, **Laura E. Young**, is a professional editor, communications specialist, and author of *Solo, Yet Never Alone: Swimming the Great Lakes*! She has recently been published in an anthology, *Along the 46th*. She can be reached through Twitter: @LauraEYoung 2.

Kim Fahner, my second editor and an amazing high school English teacher, is also an accomplished and gifted poet and author in her own right! She has recently been published in an anthology, *Along the 46th*. Please check out her blog at: KimFahner. wordpress.com and she is also on Twitter:@modernirish.

Wayne Gauthier teaches at the university level in South Korea and is brilliant in his writing, editing, feedback, and thinking! His positive feedback and support help you feel that you are in capable hands. He can be reached through Twitter: @wayne_gauthier.

Joel Friedlander was a keynote speaker at the 2013 AuthorU Extravaganza and without his expert guidance and information, I would not have set up a Twitter account and taken all of his recommended first steps, which have led to this book! His website is: TheBookDesigner.com or follow him on Twitter: @JFbookman.

Joanne Kaattari is a talented author in her own right. Some of her books include: *Justice Pies: 20 Delicious & Easy Pie Recipes from the Justice Pie Project*, *Sister Soups: Recipes, Hopes and Prayers for Times of Illness*, and *Christmas Sauna Traditions*. She has been instrumental in helping me publish this book. She is Executive Director of Community Literacy of Ontario and has been working for this important non-profit organization since 1994. She loves the written word and putting her creativity into works of art! She is a member of LinkedIn and can be also be followed on Twitter: @JoanneKaattari or @SaunaStories.

Christine Schrum's knowledgeable writing feedback and supportive words are welcomed and loved! A talented poet, writer, and published author, some of her creative babies have been published in *The Atlantic, McSweeney's Internet Tendency, The Writer, A Verse Map of Vancouver, Quills Canadian Poetry,* and *Sulphur III*. She has an M.A. in writing and co-edited the poetry anthology *Leaves by Night, Flowers by Day* (2007) with Rustin Larson and Nynke Passi. Find her on Twitter: @Schrumza.

Greg Tremblay was instrumental in capturing my book concept in the video that was used for the Indiegogo campaign. He is also a talented actor, screenwriter, and musician! He can be reached at M-Potent@hotmail.com or through Twitter: @Potent_m.

Beatriz Tejeiro helped with the Indiegogo campaign. Her website is: BackerCamp.com or look for her on Twitter: @BeatrizTejeiro.

The following practitioners provide healing of body, mind, and/or spirit:

Ron Menard's life mission is to help people heal. He owns and operates Heal Inc., a zen-like restorative studio in Sudbury, Ontario, Canada. Patrons enjoy a curative 30-minute circuit including infra-red sauna, vibration machines, oxygen-infused lemon water, foot and back massagers, healing products like Chaga tea, and Himalayan salt (to name just a few). Heal Inc. also provides top-notch Registered Massage Therapist, **Christiane Corriveau**, to help the body heal. For further information, check out his Facebook page: Heal Sudbury and website: HealInc.ca.

"Real Love is the single most powerful motivator in a leader's toolbox."—Ken Blanchard, author of *The One*

Minute Manager. For twenty years, **Greg Baer**, M.D. was a highly successful surgeon, teacher, civic leader, and entrepreneur. But despite all his accomplishments, wealth, and respect, he felt empty and unhappy, which led to his near suicide. In his subsequent search for genuine happiness, he learned some principles that have changed the lives of hundreds of thousands. The mission of The Real Love Company: "We teach the real meaning of love, replacing anger and confusion with peace and confidence in individual lives and relationships." You can reach him at: greg@reallove.com, Facebook: facebook.com/TheReal LoveCompany, Twitter: @RealLoveCompany, LinkedIn: Linkedin.com/In/RealLove, and website: RealLove.com.

Klaus Buentemeyer and his partner **Karen Heilborn** operate Green Bay Lodge, a tourist resort, on spectacular Manitoulin Island, Ontario, Canada! He is a healing practitioner who has developed a signature approach to treating individuals and groups. Klaus combines his formal education as a Germany-trained Naturopathic Doctor (along with over 20 years of experience in Psychotherapeutic practice) with subtle energy work. He shares his compassion, kindness, calmness, wealth of information, and an ongoing connection to his intuitive Self with those who are open and willing to learn, heal, grow, and share. Contact them at: GreenBayLodge.com.

Traditional Chinese Medicine, in the form of Acupuncture, has been recognized for centuries as a viable healing source. **Marsha Best** and her daughter, **Crystal Best**, offer this tried-and-true modality at Magneto Therapy and Acupuncture Clinic in Azilda, Ontario, Canada. Please feel free to contact them through their website: MagnetoTherapyAcupunctureClinic.com. Their positive energy is contagious!

Dr. Adam McLeod is another gifted energy healer who helps individuals become more involved in their own healing. He is a Naturopathic Doctor, who practices in Vancouver, British Columbia, Canada. Reach him through: DreamHealer.com and YaletownNaturopathic.com.

Another healing modality that has been revolutionary and instrumental in releasing stored emotions is the work of **Dr. Bradley Nelson**, author of *The Emotion Code* and *The Body Code System*™. Visit him at his website: DrBradleyNelson.com or reach him on Twitter: @Healers Library.

These are just a few resources, but all of these qualified people are more than happy to help you be the best *you* you can be!

May you experience all the blessings that Life and Love have to share!

Sharing Love,
Paulette

About the Author

Paulette Dahl is blessed and grateful to be able to relay these messages of Love with all of you! She is an avid learner and always seeks ways to improve her most human self, so she can be her best Self to others.

She enjoys writing non-fiction, mini-plays, poetry, and humourous creative pieces. Please check out her daily Thots for the Day on Twitter: @ThotsForTheDay or her two creative writing blogs: InspiredThotsFromAnOpenMind.Blogspot.ca and Path4Peace.Blogspot.ca.

She is also the most alive and passionate when she is helping/supporting others to love who they are and own who they are becoming, through Lovin'-U-Large Life Coaching.

She is completing *Extraordinary Loving for Everyday Living Work & Play Book*. She also continues to write Love Letters for her second book, which is on relationships in the human life cycle, from conception to death.

www.ingramcontent.com/pod-product-compliance
Lightning Source LLC
Chambersburg PA
CBHW051833090426
42736CB00011B/1786